C-466   CAREER EXAMINATION SERIES

*This is your
PASSBOOK for...*

Maintainer's Helper, Group B

*Test Preparation Study Guide
Questions & Answers*

COPYRIGHT NOTICE

This book is SOLELY intended for, is sold ONLY to, and its use is RESTRICTED to individual, bona fide applicants or candidates who qualify by virtue of having seriously filed applications for appropriate license, certificate, professional and/or promotional advancement, higher school matriculation, scholarship, or other legitimate requirements of education and/or governmental authorities.

This book is NOT intended for use, class instruction, tutoring, training, duplication, copying, reprinting, excerption, or adaptation, etc., by:

1) Other publishers
2) Proprietors and/or Instructors of "Coaching" and/or Preparatory Courses
3) Personnel and/or Training Divisions of commercial, industrial, and governmental organizations
4) Schools, colleges, or universities and/or their departments and staffs, including teachers and other personnel
5) Testing Agencies or Bureaus
6) Study groups which seek by the purchase of a single volume to copy and/or duplicate and/or adapt this material for use by the group as a whole without having purchased individual volumes for each of the members of the group
7) Et al.

Such persons would be in violation of appropriate Federal and State statutes.

PROVISION OF LICENSING AGREEMENTS – Recognized educational, commercial, industrial, and governmental institutions and organizations, and others legitimately engaged in educational pursuits, including training, testing, and measurement activities, may address request for a licensing agreement to the copyright owners, who will determine whether, and under what conditions, including fees and charges, the materials in this book may be used them. In other words, a licensing facility exists for the legitimate use of the material in this book on other than an individual basis. However, it is asseverated and affirmed here that the material in this book CANNOT be used without the receipt of the express permission of such a licensing agreement from the Publishers. Inquiries re licensing should be addressed to the company, attention rights and permissions department.

All rights reserved, including the right of reproduction in whole or in part, in any form or by any means, electronic or mechanical, including photocopying, recording, or by any information storage and retrieval system, without permission in writing from the Publisher.

Copyright © 2024 by
National Learning Corporation

212 Michael Drive, Syosset, NY 11791
(516) 921-8888 • www.passbooks.com
E-mail: info@passbooks.com

PUBLISHED IN THE UNITED STATES OF AMERICA

PASSBOOK® SERIES

THE *PASSBOOK® SERIES* has been created to prepare applicants and candidates for the ultimate academic battlefield – the examination room.

At some time in our lives, each and every one of us may be required to take an examination – for validation, matriculation, admission, qualification, registration, certification, or licensure.

Based on the assumption that every applicant or candidate has met the basic formal educational standards, has taken the required number of courses, and read the necessary texts, the *PASSBOOK® SERIES* furnishes the one special preparation which may assure passing with confidence, instead of failing with insecurity. Examination questions – together with answers – are furnished as the basic vehicle for study so that the mysteries of the examination and its compounding difficulties may be eliminated or diminished by a sure method.

This book is meant to help you pass your examination provided that you qualify and are serious in your objective.

The entire field is reviewed through the huge store of content information which is succinctly presented through a provocative and challenging approach – the question-and-answer method.

A climate of success is established by furnishing the correct answers at the end of each test.

You soon learn to recognize types of questions, forms of questions, and patterns of questioning. You may even begin to anticipate expected outcomes.

You perceive that many questions are repeated or adapted so that you can gain acute insights, which may enable you to score many sure points.

You learn how to confront new questions, or types of questions, and to attack them confidently and work out the correct answers.

You note objectives and emphases, and recognize pitfalls and dangers, so that you may make positive educational adjustments.

Moreover, you are kept fully informed in relation to new concepts, methods, practices, and directions in the field.

You discover that you are actually taking the examination all the time: you are preparing for the examination by "taking" an examination, not by reading extraneous and/or supererogatory textbooks.

In short, this PASSBOOK®, used directedly, should be an important factor in helping you to pass your test.

MAINTAINER'S HELPER - GROUP B

WHAT THE JOB INVOLVES:

Maintainers Helpers - Group B assist in the maintenance, installation, inspection, testing, alteration and repair of bus and other automotive electro-mechanical equipment; clean and lubricate bus parts; move bus parts and equipment using forklifts, hi-los, hoists, hand trucks and conveyors; remove and replace worn bearing races; measure tire pressure and change flat tires; check and maintain fluid levels of engine oil, batteries, radiator and windshield washer reservoirs; fuel buses; drain waste oil; sandblast parts; drive buses and trucks; and perform related work.

SCOPE OF THE EXAMINATION:

The written test may include questions on general automotive theory, the proper selection and use of hand and power tools and equipment employed in the maintenance and repair of mechanical and electromechanical equipment; safe work practices in repair and maintenance shops for mechanical and electro-mechanical equipment; reading and interpreting written instructions; reading meters; taking measurements and basic shop computations; basic electrical and mechanical theory; and other related areas.

HOW TO TAKE A TEST

I. YOU MUST PASS AN EXAMINATION

A. WHAT EVERY CANDIDATE SHOULD KNOW

Examination applicants often ask us for help in preparing for the written test. What can I study in advance? What kinds of questions will be asked? How will the test be given? How will the papers be graded?

As an applicant for a civil service examination, you may be wondering about some of these things. Our purpose here is to suggest effective methods of advance study and to describe civil service examinations.

Your chances for success on this examination can be increased if you know how to prepare. Those "pre-examination jitters" can be reduced if you know what to expect. You can even experience an adventure in good citizenship if you know why civil service exams are given.

B. WHY ARE CIVIL SERVICE EXAMINATIONS GIVEN?

Civil service examinations are important to you in two ways. As a citizen, you want public jobs filled by employees who know how to do their work. As a job seeker, you want a fair chance to compete for that job on an equal footing with other candidates. The best-known means of accomplishing this two-fold goal is the competitive examination.

Exams are widely publicized throughout the nation. They may be administered for jobs in federal, state, city, municipal, town or village governments or agencies.

Any citizen may apply, with some limitations, such as the age or residence of applicants. Your experience and education may be reviewed to see whether you meet the requirements for the particular examination. When these requirements exist, they are reasonable and applied consistently to all applicants. Thus, a competitive examination may cause you some uneasiness now, but it is your privilege and safeguard.

C. HOW ARE CIVIL SERVICE EXAMS DEVELOPED?

Examinations are carefully written by trained technicians who are specialists in the field known as "psychological measurement," in consultation with recognized authorities in the field of work that the test will cover. These experts recommend the subject matter areas or skills to be tested; only those knowledges or skills important to your success on the job are included. The most reliable books and source materials available are used as references. Together, the experts and technicians judge the difficulty level of the questions.

Test technicians know how to phrase questions so that the problem is clearly stated. Their ethics do not permit "trick" or "catch" questions. Questions may have been tried out on sample groups, or subjected to statistical analysis, to determine their usefulness.

Written tests are often used in combination with performance tests, ratings of training and experience, and oral interviews. All of these measures combine to form the best-known means of finding the right person for the right job.

II. HOW TO PASS THE WRITTEN TEST

A. NATURE OF THE EXAMINATION

To prepare intelligently for civil service examinations, you should know how they differ from school examinations you have taken. In school you were assigned certain definite pages to read or subjects to cover. The examination questions were quite detailed and usually emphasized memory. Civil service exams, on the other hand, try to discover your present ability to perform the duties of a position, plus your potentiality to learn these duties. In other words, a civil service exam attempts to predict how successful you will be. Questions cover such a broad area that they cannot be as minute and detailed as school exam questions.

In the public service similar kinds of work, or positions, are grouped together in one "class." This process is known as *position-classification*. All the positions in a class are paid according to the salary range for that class. One class title covers all of these positions, and they are all tested by the same examination.

B. FOUR BASIC STEPS

1) Study the announcement

How, then, can you know what subjects to study? Our best answer is: "Learn as much as possible about the class of positions for which you've applied." The exam will test the knowledge, skills and abilities needed to do the work.

Your most valuable source of information about the position you want is the official exam announcement. This announcement lists the training and experience qualifications. Check these standards and apply only if you come reasonably close to meeting them.

The brief description of the position in the examination announcement offers some clues to the subjects which will be tested. Think about the job itself. Review the duties in your mind. Can you perform them, or are there some in which you are rusty? Fill in the blank spots in your preparation.

Many jurisdictions preview the written test in the exam announcement by including a section called "Knowledge and Abilities Required," "Scope of the Examination," or some similar heading. Here you will find out specifically what fields will be tested.

2) Review your own background

Once you learn in general what the position is all about, and what you need to know to do the work, ask yourself which subjects you already know fairly well and which need improvement. You may wonder whether to concentrate on improving your strong areas or on building some background in your fields of weakness. When the announcement has specified "some knowledge" or "considerable knowledge," or has used adjectives like "beginning principles of..." or "advanced ... methods," you can get a clue as to the number and difficulty of questions to be asked in any given field. More questions, and hence broader coverage, would be included for those subjects which are more important in the work. Now weigh your strengths and weaknesses against the job requirements and prepare accordingly.

3) Determine the level of the position

Another way to tell how intensively you should prepare is to understand the level of the job for which you are applying. Is it the entering level? In other words, is this the position in which beginners in a field of work are hired? Or is it an intermediate or advanced level? Sometimes this is indicated by such words as "Junior" or "Senior" in the class title. Other jurisdictions use Roman numerals to designate the level – Clerk I, Clerk II, for example. The word "Supervisor" sometimes appears in the title. If the level is not indicated by the title, check the description of duties. Will you be working under very close supervision, or will you have responsibility for independent decisions in this work?

4) Choose appropriate study materials

Now that you know the subjects to be examined and the relative amount of each subject to be covered, you can choose suitable study materials. For beginning level jobs, or even advanced ones, if you have a pronounced weakness in some aspect of your training, read a modern, standard textbook in that field. Be sure it is up to date and has general coverage. Such books are normally available at your library, and the librarian will be glad to help you locate one. For entry-level positions, questions of appropriate difficulty are chosen – neither highly advanced questions, nor those too simple. Such questions require careful thought but not advanced training.

If the position for which you are applying is technical or advanced, you will read more advanced, specialized material. If you are already familiar with the basic principles of your field, elementary textbooks would waste your time. Concentrate on advanced textbooks and technical periodicals. Think through the concepts and review difficult problems in your field.

These are all general sources. You can get more ideas on your own initiative, following these leads. For example, training manuals and publications of the government agency which employs workers in your field can be useful, particularly for technical and professional positions. A letter or visit to the government department involved may result in more specific study suggestions, and certainly will provide you with a more definite idea of the exact nature of the position you are seeking.

III. KINDS OF TESTS

Tests are used for purposes other than measuring knowledge and ability to perform specified duties. For some positions, it is equally important to test ability to make adjustments to new situations or to profit from training. In others, basic mental abilities not dependent on information are essential. Questions which test these things may not appear as pertinent to the duties of the position as those which test for knowledge and information. Yet they are often highly important parts of a fair examination. For very general questions, it is almost impossible to help you direct your study efforts. What we can do is to point out some of the more common of these general abilities needed in public service positions and describe some typical questions.

1) General information

Broad, general information has been found useful for predicting job success in some kinds of work. This is tested in a variety of ways, from vocabulary lists to questions about current events. Basic background in some field of work, such as sociology or economics, may be sampled in a group of questions. Often these are principles which have become familiar to most persons through exposure rather than through formal training. It is difficult to advise you how to study for these questions; being alert to the world around you is our best suggestion.

2) Verbal ability

An example of an ability needed in many positions is verbal or language ability. Verbal ability is, in brief, the ability to use and understand words. Vocabulary and grammar tests are typical measures of this ability. Reading comprehension or paragraph interpretation questions are common in many kinds of civil service tests. You are given a paragraph of written material and asked to find its central meaning.

3) Numerical ability

Number skills can be tested by the familiar arithmetic problem, by checking paired lists of numbers to see which are alike and which are different, or by interpreting charts and graphs. In the latter test, a graph may be printed in the test booklet which you are asked to use as the basis for answering questions.

4) Observation

A popular test for law-enforcement positions is the observation test. A picture is shown to you for several minutes, then taken away. Questions about the picture test your ability to observe both details and larger elements.

5) Following directions

In many positions in the public service, the employee must be able to carry out written instructions dependably and accurately. You may be given a chart with several columns, each column listing a variety of information. The questions require you to carry out directions involving the information given in the chart.

6) Skills and aptitudes

Performance tests effectively measure some manual skills and aptitudes. When the skill is one in which you are trained, such as typing or shorthand, you can practice. These tests are often very much like those given in business school or high school courses. For many of the other skills and aptitudes, however, no short-time preparation can be made. Skills and abilities natural to you or that you have developed throughout your lifetime are being tested.

Many of the general questions just described provide all the data needed to answer the questions and ask you to use your reasoning ability to find the answers. Your best preparation for these tests, as well as for tests of facts and ideas, is to be at your physical and mental best. You, no doubt, have your own methods of getting into an exam-taking mood and keeping "in shape." The next section lists some ideas on this subject.

IV. KINDS OF QUESTIONS

Only rarely is the "essay" question, which you answer in narrative form, used in civil service tests. Civil service tests are usually of the short-answer type. Full instructions for answering these questions will be given to you at the examination. But in case this is your first experience with short-answer questions and separate answer sheets, here is what you need to know:

1) **Multiple-choice Questions**

Most popular of the short-answer questions is the "multiple choice" or "best answer" question. It can be used, for example, to test for factual knowledge, ability to solve problems or judgment in meeting situations found at work.

A multiple-choice question is normally one of three types—
- It can begin with an incomplete statement followed by several possible endings. You are to find the one ending which *best* completes the statement, although some of the others may not be entirely wrong.
- It can also be a complete statement in the form of a question which is answered by choosing one of the statements listed.

- It can be in the form of a problem – again you select the best answer.

Here is an example of a multiple-choice question with a discussion which should give you some clues as to the method for choosing the right answer:

When an employee has a complaint about his assignment, the action which will *best* help him overcome his difficulty is to
- A. discuss his difficulty with his coworkers
- B. take the problem to the head of the organization
- C. take the problem to the person who gave him the assignment
- D. say nothing to anyone about his complaint

In answering this question, you should study each of the choices to find which is best. Consider choice "A" – Certainly an employee may discuss his complaint with fellow employees, but no change or improvement can result, and the complaint remains unresolved. Choice "B" is a poor choice since the head of the organization probably does not know what assignment you have been given, and taking your problem to him is known as "going over the head" of the supervisor. The supervisor, or person who made the assignment, is the person who can clarify it or correct any injustice. Choice "C" is, therefore, correct. To say nothing, as in choice "D," is unwise. Supervisors have and interest in knowing the problems employees are facing, and the employee is seeking a solution to his problem.

2) True/False Questions

The "true/false" or "right/wrong" form of question is sometimes used. Here a complete statement is given. Your job is to decide whether the statement is right or wrong.

SAMPLE: A roaming cell-phone call to a nearby city costs less than a non-roaming call to a distant city.

This statement is wrong, or false, since roaming calls are more expensive.

This is not a complete list of all possible question forms, although most of the others are variations of these common types. You will always get complete directions for answering questions. Be sure you understand *how* to mark your answers – ask questions until you do.

V. RECORDING YOUR ANSWERS

Computer terminals are used more and more today for many different kinds of exams.
For an examination with very few applicants, you may be told to record your answers in the test booklet itself. Separate answer sheets are much more common. If this separate answer sheet is to be scored by machine – and this is often the case – it is highly important that you mark your answers correctly in order to get credit.

An electronic scoring machine is often used in civil service offices because of the speed with which papers can be scored. Machine-scored answer sheets must be marked with a pencil, which will be given to you. This pencil has a high graphite content which responds to the electronic scoring machine. As a matter of fact, stray dots may register as answers, so do not let your pencil rest on the answer sheet while you are pondering the correct answer. Also, if your pencil lead breaks or is otherwise defective, ask for another.

Since the answer sheet will be dropped in a slot in the scoring machine, be careful not to bend the corners or get the paper crumpled.

The answer sheet normally has five vertical columns of numbers, with 30 numbers to a column. These numbers correspond to the question numbers in your test booklet. After each number, going across the page are four or five pairs of dotted lines. These short dotted lines have small letters or numbers above them. The first two pairs may also have a "T" or "F" above the letters. This indicates that the first two pairs only are to be used if the questions are of the true-false type. If the questions are multiple choice, disregard the "T" and "F" and pay attention only to the small letters or numbers.

Answer your questions in the manner of the sample that follows:

32. The largest city in the United States is
    A. Washington, D.C.
    B. New York City
    C. Chicago
    D. Detroit
    E. San Francisco

1) Choose the answer you think is best. (New York City is the largest, so "B" is correct.)
2) Find the row of dotted lines numbered the same as the question you are answering. (Find row number 32)
3) Find the pair of dotted lines corresponding to the answer. (Find the pair of lines under the mark "B.")
4) Make a solid black mark between the dotted lines.

VI. BEFORE THE TEST

Common sense will help you find procedures to follow to get ready for an examination. Too many of us, however, overlook these sensible measures. Indeed, nervousness and fatigue have been found to be the most serious reasons why applicants fail to do their best on civil service tests. Here is a list of reminders:

- Begin your preparation early – Don't wait until the last minute to go scurrying around for books and materials or to find out what the position is all about.
- Prepare continuously – An hour a night for a week is better than an all-night cram session. This has been definitely established. What is more, a night a week for a month will return better dividends than crowding your study into a shorter period of time.
- Locate the place of the exam – You have been sent a notice telling you when and where to report for the examination. If the location is in a different town or otherwise unfamiliar to you, it would be well to inquire the best route and learn something about the building.
- Relax the night before the test – Allow your mind to rest. Do not study at all that night. Plan some mild recreation or diversion; then go to bed early and get a good night's sleep.
- Get up early enough to make a leisurely trip to the place for the test – This way unforeseen events, traffic snarls, unfamiliar buildings, etc. will not upset you.
- Dress comfortably – A written test is not a fashion show. You will be known by number and not by name, so wear something comfortable.

- Leave excess paraphernalia at home – Shopping bags and odd bundles will get in your way. You need bring only the items mentioned in the official notice you received; usually everything you need is provided. Do not bring reference books to the exam. They will only confuse those last minutes and be taken away from you when in the test room.
- Arrive somewhat ahead of time – If because of transportation schedules you must get there very early, bring a newspaper or magazine to take your mind off yourself while waiting.
- Locate the examination room – When you have found the proper room, you will be directed to the seat or part of the room where you will sit. Sometimes you are given a sheet of instructions to read while you are waiting. Do not fill out any forms until you are told to do so; just read them and be prepared.
- Relax and prepare to listen to the instructions
- If you have any physical problem that may keep you from doing your best, be sure to tell the test administrator. If you are sick or in poor health, you really cannot do your best on the exam. You can come back and take the test some other time.

VII. AT THE TEST

The day of the test is here and you have the test booklet in your hand. The temptation to get going is very strong. Caution! There is more to success than knowing the right answers. You must know how to identify your papers and understand variations in the type of short-answer question used in this particular examination. Follow these suggestions for maximum results from your efforts:

1) Cooperate with the monitor

The test administrator has a duty to create a situation in which you can be as much at ease as possible. He will give instructions, tell you when to begin, check to see that you are marking your answer sheet correctly, and so on. He is not there to guard you, although he will see that your competitors do not take unfair advantage. He wants to help you do your best.

2) Listen to all instructions

Don't jump the gun! Wait until you understand all directions. In most civil service tests you get more time than you need to answer the questions. So don't be in a hurry. Read each word of instructions until you clearly understand the meaning. Study the examples, listen to all announcements and follow directions. Ask questions if you do not understand what to do.

3) Identify your papers

Civil service exams are usually identified by number only. You will be assigned a number; you must not put your name on your test papers. Be sure to copy your number correctly. Since more than one exam may be given, copy your exact examination title.

4) Plan your time

Unless you are told that a test is a "speed" or "rate of work" test, speed itself is usually not important. Time enough to answer all the questions will be provided, but this does not mean that you have all day. An overall time limit has been set. Divide the total time (in minutes) by the number of questions to determine the approximate time you have for each question.

5) Do not linger over difficult questions

If you come across a difficult question, mark it with a paper clip (useful to have along) and come back to it when you have been through the booklet. One caution if you do this – be sure to skip a number on your answer sheet as well. Check often to be sure that you have not lost your place and that you are marking in the row numbered the same as the question you are answering.

6) Read the questions

Be sure you know what the question asks! Many capable people are unsuccessful because they failed to *read* the questions correctly.

7) Answer all questions

Unless you have been instructed that a penalty will be deducted for incorrect answers, it is better to guess than to omit a question.

8) Speed tests

It is often better NOT to guess on speed tests. It has been found that on timed tests people are tempted to spend the last few seconds before time is called in marking answers at random – without even reading them – in the hope of picking up a few extra points. To discourage this practice, the instructions may warn you that your score will be "corrected" for guessing. That is, a penalty will be applied. The incorrect answers will be deducted from the correct ones, or some other penalty formula will be used.

9) Review your answers

If you finish before time is called, go back to the questions you guessed or omitted to give them further thought. Review other answers if you have time.

10) Return your test materials

If you are ready to leave before others have finished or time is called, take ALL your materials to the monitor and leave quietly. Never take any test material with you. The monitor can discover whose papers are not complete, and taking a test booklet may be grounds for disqualification.

VIII. EXAMINATION TECHNIQUES

1) Read the general instructions carefully. These are usually printed on the first page of the exam booklet. As a rule, these instructions refer to the timing of the examination; the fact that you should not start work until the signal and must stop work at a signal, etc. If there are any *special* instructions, such as a choice of questions to be answered, make sure that you note this instruction carefully.

2) When you are ready to start work on the examination, that is as soon as the signal has been given, read the instructions to each question booklet, underline any key words or phrases, such as *least, best, outline, describe* and the like. In this way you will tend to answer as requested rather than discover on reviewing your paper that you *listed without describing*, that you selected the *worst* choice rather than the *best* choice, etc.

3) If the examination is of the objective or multiple-choice type – that is, each question will also give a series of possible answers: A, B, C or D, and you are called upon to select the best answer and write the letter next to that answer on your answer paper – it is advisable to start answering each question in turn. There may be anywhere from 50 to 100 such questions in the three or four hours allotted and you can see how much time would be taken if you read through all the questions before beginning to answer any. Furthermore, if you come across a question or group of questions which you know would be difficult to answer, it would undoubtedly affect your handling of all the other questions.

4) If the examination is of the essay type and contains but a few questions, it is a moot point as to whether you should read all the questions before starting to answer any one. Of course, if you are given a choice – say five out of seven and the like – then it is essential to read all the questions so you can eliminate the two that are most difficult. If, however, you are asked to answer all the questions, there may be danger in trying to answer the easiest one first because you may find that you will spend too much time on it. The best technique is to answer the first question, then proceed to the second, etc.

5) Time your answers. Before the exam begins, write down the time it started, then add the time allowed for the examination and write down the time it must be completed, then divide the time available somewhat as follows:
   - If 3-1/2 hours are allowed, that would be 210 minutes. If you have 80 objective-type questions, that would be an average of 2-1/2 minutes per question. Allow yourself no more than 2 minutes per question, or a total of 160 minutes, which will permit about 50 minutes to review.
   - If for the time allotment of 210 minutes there are 7 essay questions to answer, that would average about 30 minutes a question. Give yourself only 25 minutes per question so that you have about 35 minutes to review.

6) The most important instruction is to *read each question* and make sure you know what is wanted. The second most important instruction is to *time yourself properly* so that you answer every question. The third most important instruction is to *answer every question*. Guess if you have to but include something for each question. Remember that you will receive no credit for a blank and will probably receive some credit if you write something in answer to an essay question. If you guess a letter – say "B" for a multiple-choice question – you may have guessed right. If you leave a blank as an answer to a multiple-choice question, the examiners may respect your feelings but it will not add a point to your score. Some exams may penalize you for wrong answers, so in such cases *only*, you may not want to guess unless you have some basis for your answer.

7) Suggestions
   a. Objective-type questions
      1. Examine the question booklet for proper sequence of pages and questions
      2. Read all instructions carefully
      3. Skip any question which seems too difficult; return to it after all other questions have been answered
      4. Apportion your time properly; do not spend too much time on any single question or group of questions

5. Note and underline key words – *all, most, fewest, least, best, worst, same, opposite,* etc.
6. Pay particular attention to negatives
7. Note unusual option, e.g., unduly long, short, complex, different or similar in content to the body of the question
8. Observe the use of "hedging" words – *probably, may, most likely,* etc.
9. Make sure that your answer is put next to the same number as the question
10. Do not second-guess unless you have good reason to believe the second answer is definitely more correct
11. Cross out original answer if you decide another answer is more accurate; do not erase until you are ready to hand your paper in
12. Answer all questions; guess unless instructed otherwise
13. Leave time for review

b. Essay questions
1. Read each question carefully
2. Determine exactly what is wanted. Underline key words or phrases.
3. Decide on outline or paragraph answer
4. Include many different points and elements unless asked to develop any one or two points or elements
5. Show impartiality by giving pros and cons unless directed to select one side only
6. Make and write down any assumptions you find necessary to answer the questions
7. Watch your English, grammar, punctuation and choice of words
8. Time your answers; don't crowd material

8) Answering the essay question

Most essay questions can be answered by framing the specific response around several key words or ideas. Here are a few such key words or ideas:

M's: manpower, materials, methods, money, management
P's: purpose, program, policy, plan, procedure, practice, problems, pitfalls, personnel, public relations

a. Six basic steps in handling problems:
1. Preliminary plan and background development
2. Collect information, data and facts
3. Analyze and interpret information, data and facts
4. Analyze and develop solutions as well as make recommendations
5. Prepare report and sell recommendations
6. Install recommendations and follow up effectiveness

b. Pitfalls to avoid
1. *Taking things for granted* – A statement of the situation does not necessarily imply that each of the elements is necessarily true; for example, a complaint may be invalid and biased so that all that can be taken for granted is that a complaint has been registered

2. *Considering only one side of a situation* – Wherever possible, indicate several alternatives and then point out the reasons you selected the best one
3. *Failing to indicate follow up* – Whenever your answer indicates action on your part, make certain that you will take proper follow-up action to see how successful your recommendations, procedures or actions turn out to be
4. *Taking too long in answering any single question* – Remember to time your answers properly

IX. AFTER THE TEST

Scoring procedures differ in detail among civil service jurisdictions although the general principles are the same. Whether the papers are hand-scored or graded by machine we have described, they are nearly always graded by number. That is, the person who marks the paper knows only the number – never the name – of the applicant. Not until all the papers have been graded will they be matched with names. If other tests, such as training and experience or oral interview ratings have been given, scores will be combined. Different parts of the examination usually have different weights. For example, the written test might count 60 percent of the final grade, and a rating of training and experience 40 percent. In many jurisdictions, veterans will have a certain number of points added to their grades.

After the final grade has been determined, the names are placed in grade order and an eligible list is established. There are various methods for resolving ties between those who get the same final grade – probably the most common is to place first the name of the person whose application was received first. Job offers are made from the eligible list in the order the names appear on it. You will be notified of your grade and your rank as soon as all these computations have been made. This will be done as rapidly as possible.

People who are found to meet the requirements in the announcement are called "eligibles." Their names are put on a list of eligible candidates. An eligible's chances of getting a job depend on how high he stands on this list and how fast agencies are filling jobs from the list.

When a job is to be filled from a list of eligibles, the agency asks for the names of people on the list of eligibles for that job. When the civil service commission receives this request, it sends to the agency the names of the three people highest on this list. Or, if the job to be filled has specialized requirements, the office sends the agency the names of the top three persons who meet these requirements from the general list.

The appointing officer makes a choice from among the three people whose names were sent to him. If the selected person accepts the appointment, the names of the others are put back on the list to be considered for future openings.

That is the rule in hiring from all kinds of eligible lists, whether they are for typist, carpenter, chemist, or something else. For every vacancy, the appointing officer has his choice of any one of the top three eligibles on the list. This explains why the person whose name is on top of the list sometimes does not get an appointment when some of the persons lower on the list do. If the appointing officer chooses the second or third eligible, the No. 1 eligible does not get a job at once, but stays on the list until he is appointed or the list is terminated.

X. HOW TO PASS THE INTERVIEW TEST

The examination for which you applied requires an oral interview test. You have already taken the written test and you are now being called for the interview test – the final part of the formal examination.

You may think that it is not possible to prepare for an interview test and that there are no procedures to follow during an interview. Our purpose is to point out some things you can do in advance that will help you and some good rules to follow and pitfalls to avoid while you are being interviewed.

What is an interview supposed to test?

The written examination is designed to test the technical knowledge and competence of the candidate; the oral is designed to evaluate intangible qualities, not readily measured otherwise, and to establish a list showing the relative fitness of each candidate – as measured against his competitors – for the position sought. Scoring is not on the basis of "right" and "wrong," but on a sliding scale of values ranging from "not passable" to "outstanding." As a matter of fact, it is possible to achieve a relatively low score without a single "incorrect" answer because of evident weakness in the qualities being measured.

Occasionally, an examination may consist entirely of an oral test – either an individual or a group oral. In such cases, information is sought concerning the technical knowledges and abilities of the candidate, since there has been no written examination for this purpose. More commonly, however, an oral test is used to supplement a written examination.

Who conducts interviews?

The composition of oral boards varies among different jurisdictions. In nearly all, a representative of the personnel department serves as chairman. One of the members of the board may be a representative of the department in which the candidate would work. In some cases, "outside experts" are used, and, frequently, a businessman or some other representative of the general public is asked to serve. Labor and management or other special groups may be represented. The aim is to secure the services of experts in the appropriate field.

However the board is composed, it is a good idea (and not at all improper or unethical) to ascertain in advance of the interview who the members are and what groups they represent. When you are introduced to them, you will have some idea of their backgrounds and interests, and at least you will not stutter and stammer over their names.

What should be done before the interview?

While knowledge about the board members is useful and takes some of the surprise element out of the interview, there is other preparation which is more substantive. It *is* possible to prepare for an oral interview – in several ways:

1) Keep a copy of your application and review it carefully before the interview

This may be the only document before the oral board, and the starting point of the interview. Know what education and experience you have listed there, and the sequence and dates of all of it. Sometimes the board will ask you to review the highlights of your experience for them; you should not have to hem and haw doing it.

2) Study the class specification and the examination announcement

Usually, the oral board has one or both of these to guide them. The qualities, characteristics or knowledges required by the position sought are stated in these documents. They offer valuable clues as to the nature of the oral interview. For example, if the job involves supervisory responsibilities, the announcement will usually indicate that knowledge of modern supervisory methods and the qualifications of the candidate as a supervisor will be tested. If so, you can expect such questions, frequently in the form of a hypothetical situation which you are expected to solve. NEVER go into an oral without knowledge of the duties and responsibilities of the job you seek.

3) Think through each qualification required

Try to visualize the kind of questions you would ask if you were a board member. How well could you answer them? Try especially to appraise your own knowledge and background in each area, *measured against the job sought*, and identify any areas in which you are weak. Be critical and realistic – do not flatter yourself.

4) Do some general reading in areas in which you feel you may be weak

For example, if the job involves supervision and your past experience has NOT, some general reading in supervisory methods and practices, particularly in the field of human relations, might be useful. Do NOT study agency procedures or detailed manuals. The oral board will be testing your understanding and capacity, not your memory.

5) Get a good night's sleep and watch your general health and mental attitude

You will want a clear head at the interview. Take care of a cold or any other minor ailment, and of course, no hangovers.

What should be done on the day of the interview?

Now comes the day of the interview itself. Give yourself plenty of time to get there. Plan to arrive somewhat ahead of the scheduled time, particularly if your appointment is in the fore part of the day. If a previous candidate fails to appear, the board might be ready for you a bit early. By early afternoon an oral board is almost invariably behind schedule if there are many candidates, and you may have to wait. Take along a book or magazine to read, or your application to review, but leave any extraneous material in the waiting room when you go in for your interview. In any event, relax and compose yourself.

The matter of dress is important. The board is forming impressions about you – from your experience, your manners, your attitude, and your appearance. Give your personal appearance careful attention. Dress your best, but not your flashiest. Choose conservative, appropriate clothing, and be sure it is immaculate. This is a business interview, and your appearance should indicate that you regard it as such. Besides, being well groomed and properly dressed will help boost your confidence.

Sooner or later, someone will call your name and escort you into the interview room. *This is it.* From here on you are on your own. It is too late for any more preparation. But remember, you asked for this opportunity to prove your fitness, and you are here because your request was granted.

What happens when you go in?

The usual sequence of events will be as follows: The clerk (who is often the board stenographer) will introduce you to the chairman of the oral board, who will introduce you to the other members of the board. Acknowledge the introductions before you sit down. Do not be surprised if you find a microphone facing you or a stenotypist sitting by. Oral interviews are usually recorded in the event of an appeal or other review.

Usually the chairman of the board will open the interview by reviewing the highlights of your education and work experience from your application – primarily for the benefit of the other members of the board, as well as to get the material into the record. Do not interrupt or comment unless there is an error or significant misinterpretation; if that is the case, do not hesitate. But do not quibble about insignificant matters. Also, he will usually ask you some question about your education, experience or your present job – partly to get you to start talking and to establish the interviewing "rapport." He may start the actual questioning, or turn it over to one of the other members. Frequently, each member undertakes the questioning on a particular area, one in which he is perhaps most competent, so you can expect each member to participate in the examination. Because time is limited, you may also expect some rather abrupt switches in the direction the questioning takes, so do not be upset by it. Normally, a board member will not pursue a single line of questioning unless he discovers a particular strength or weakness.

After each member has participated, the chairman will usually ask whether any member has any further questions, then will ask you if you have anything you wish to add. Unless you are expecting this question, it may floor you. Worse, it may start you off on an extended, extemporaneous speech. The board is not usually seeking more information. The question is principally to offer you a last opportunity to present further qualifications or to indicate that you have nothing to add. So, if you feel that a significant qualification or characteristic has been overlooked, it is proper to point it out in a sentence or so. Do not compliment the board on the thoroughness of their examination – they have been sketchy, and you know it. If you wish, merely say, "No thank you, I have nothing further to add." This is a point where you can "talk yourself out" of a good impression or fail to present an important bit of information. Remember, *you close the interview yourself.*

The chairman will then say, "That is all, Mr. _____, thank you." Do not be startled; the interview is over, and quicker than you think. Thank him, gather your belongings and take your leave. Save your sigh of relief for the other side of the door.

How to put your best foot forward

Throughout this entire process, you may feel that the board individually and collectively is trying to pierce your defenses, seek out your hidden weaknesses and embarrass and confuse you. Actually, this is not true. They are obliged to make an appraisal of your qualifications for the job you are seeking, and they want to see you in your best light. Remember, they must interview all candidates and a non-cooperative candidate may become a failure in spite of their best efforts to bring out his qualifications. Here are 15 suggestions that will help you:

1) Be natural – Keep your attitude confident, not cocky

If you are not confident that you can do the job, do not expect the board to be. Do not apologize for your weaknesses, try to bring out your strong points. The board is interested in a positive, not negative, presentation. Cockiness will antagonize any board member and make him wonder if you are covering up a weakness by a false show of strength.

2) Get comfortable, but don't lounge or sprawl

Sit erectly but not stiffly. A careless posture may lead the board to conclude that you are careless in other things, or at least that you are not impressed by the importance of the occasion. Either conclusion is natural, even if incorrect. Do not fuss with your clothing, a pencil or an ashtray. Your hands may occasionally be useful to emphasize a point; do not let them become a point of distraction.

3) Do not wisecrack or make small talk

This is a serious situation, and your attitude should show that you consider it as such. Further, the time of the board is limited – they do not want to waste it, and neither should you.

4) Do not exaggerate your experience or abilities

In the first place, from information in the application or other interviews and sources, the board may know more about you than you think. Secondly, you probably will not get away with it. An experienced board is rather adept at spotting such a situation, so do not take the chance.

5) If you know a board member, do not make a point of it, yet do not hide it

Certainly you are not fooling him, and probably not the other members of the board. Do not try to take advantage of your acquaintanceship – it will probably do you little good.

6) Do not dominate the interview

Let the board do that. They will give you the clues – do not assume that you have to do all the talking. Realize that the board has a number of questions to ask you, and do not try to take up all the interview time by showing off your extensive knowledge of the answer to the first one.

7) Be attentive

You only have 20 minutes or so, and you should keep your attention at its sharpest throughout. When a member is addressing a problem or question to you, give him your undivided attention. Address your reply principally to him, but do not exclude the other board members.

8) Do not interrupt

A board member may be stating a problem for you to analyze. He will ask you a question when the time comes. Let him state the problem, and wait for the question.

9) Make sure you understand the question

Do not try to answer until you are sure what the question is. If it is not clear, restate it in your own words or ask the board member to clarify it for you. However, do not haggle about minor elements.

10) Reply promptly but not hastily

A common entry on oral board rating sheets is "candidate responded readily," or "candidate hesitated in replies." Respond as promptly and quickly as you can, but do not jump to a hasty, ill-considered answer.

11) Do not be peremptory in your answers

A brief answer is proper – but do not fire your answer back. That is a losing game from your point of view. The board member can probably ask questions much faster than you can answer them.

12) Do not try to create the answer you think the board member wants

He is interested in what kind of mind you have and how it works – not in playing games. Furthermore, he can usually spot this practice and will actually grade you down on it.

13) Do not switch sides in your reply merely to agree with a board member

Frequently, a member will take a contrary position merely to draw you out and to see if you are willing and able to defend your point of view. Do not start a debate, yet do not surrender a good position. If a position is worth taking, it is worth defending.

14) Do not be afraid to admit an error in judgment if you are shown to be wrong

The board knows that you are forced to reply without any opportunity for careful consideration. Your answer may be demonstrably wrong. If so, admit it and get on with the interview.

15) Do not dwell at length on your present job

The opening question may relate to your present assignment. Answer the question but do not go into an extended discussion. You are being examined for a *new* job, not your present one. As a matter of fact, try to phrase ALL your answers in terms of the job for which you are being examined.

Basis of Rating

Probably you will forget most of these "do's" and "don'ts" when you walk into the oral interview room. Even remembering them all will not ensure you a passing grade. Perhaps you did not have the qualifications in the first place. But remembering them will help you to put your best foot forward, without treading on the toes of the board members.

Rumor and popular opinion to the contrary notwithstanding, an oral board wants you to make the best appearance possible. They know you are under pressure – but they also want to see how you respond to it as a guide to what your reaction would be under the pressures of the job you seek. They will be influenced by the degree of poise you display, the personal traits you show and the manner in which you respond.

ABOUT THIS BOOK

This book contains tests divided into Examination Sections. Go through each test, answering every question in the margin. We have also attached a sample answer sheet at the back of the book that can be removed and used. At the end of each test look at the answer key and check your answers. On the ones you got wrong, look at the right answer choice and learn. Do not fill in the answers first. Do not memorize the questions and answers, but understand the answer and principles involved. On your test, the questions will likely be different from the samples. Questions are changed and new ones added. If you understand these past questions you should have success with any changes that arise. Tests may consist of several types of questions. We have additional books on each subject should more study be advisable or necessary for you. Finally, the more you study, the better prepared you will be. This book is intended to be the last thing you study before you walk into the examination room. Prior study of relevant texts is also recommended. NLC publishes some of these in our Fundamental Series. Knowledge and good sense are important factors in passing your exam. Good luck also helps. So now study this Passbook, absorb the material contained within and take that knowledge into the examination. Then do your best to pass that exam.

EXAMINATION SECTION

EXAMINATION SECTION

TEST 1

DIRECTIONS: Each question or incomplete statement is followed by several suggested answers or completions. Select the one that BEST answers the question or completes the statement. *PRINT THE LETTER OF THE CORRECT ANSWER IN THE SPACE AT THE RIGHT.*

1. A gap of several thousandths of an inch between two parts is MOST accurately measured with a
    A. divider
    B. feeler gage
    C. vernier caliper
    D. gage block

    1._____

2. For a very high-speed reduction the type of gear generally used is the
    A. worm and gear
    B. spur gear
    C. bevel gear
    D. herringbone gear

    2._____

3. The spiral flutes on a twist drill are provided to
    A. remove the chips
    B. form a clearance hole
    C. prevent the drill from wobbling
    D. save material

    3._____

4. The tool whose size is specified by weight is a
    A. cold chisel
    B. hammer
    C. wrench
    D. pair of pliers

    4._____

5. Ball bearings are USUALLY made of
    A. steel   B. brass   C. cast iron   D. babbit

    5._____

6. An item which has the LEAST value in promoting general shop safety is
    A. plenty of overtime
    B. safety posters
    C. skilled employees
    D. expensive equipment

    6._____

7. It would be MOST necessary to provide a metal cover for a container used for
    A. machine shop scrap
    B. floor sweepings
    C. oily rags and waste
    D. broken glass

    7._____

8. A helper is NOT expected to assume responsibility. This means that
    A. he should not report defective equipment unless asked
    B. his supervisors have a low opinion of his ability
    C. he never does important work
    D. generally other employees are assigned to make the decisions

    8._____

9. A sheet metal screw differs from an ordinary machine screw in that it   9._____
    A. requires a special nut
    B. always requires a special screwdriver
    C. is self-tapping
    D. is made only in short lengths

10. In moving heavy equipment or materials with an overhead traveling   10._____
    crane, a good procedure is to have the crane operator take operating
    signals from only a single designated person on the floor. This is
    important because it
    A. avoids the necessity of more than one person knowing the signals
    B. prevents overloading the crane with too much load
    C. requires fewer men
    D. avoids the danger of conflicting signals

11. Protective goggles should NOT be worn when   11._____
    A. descending a ladder after finishing a job
    B. dusting off machinery
    C. chipping concrete
    D. sharpening a cold chisel on a grinding wheel

12. The GREATEST danger in the use of ladders, stairways, floors and   12._____
    platforms made of iron is that they
    A. are difficult to maintain
    B. are slippery when greasy and wet
    C. have sharp edges causing injuries
    D. are too rigid and cause fatigue

13. Compressed air should NOT be used directly from a hose for dusting off   13._____
    work clothing mainly because
    A. the air may contain considerable moisture
    B. the dust may blow into machinery
    C. it may cause personal injury
    D. it is too noisy

14. The term which CORRECTLY refers to a machine screw is   14._____
    A. 8-24   B. #2 head   C. 10-penny   D. 1/2 by 3/4

15. Artificial respiration is applied when an accident has caused   15._____
    A. broken limbs   B. scalding
    C. breathing difficulties D. loss of blood

16. Lock washers are used PRINCIPALLY with   16._____
    A. wood screws   B. lag screws
    C. self-tapping screws   D. machine screws

17. All employees receive a copy of the book "Rules and Regulations." The MOST likely reason for issuing this book is to
    A. give the answers to all technical questions
    B. relieve management of responsibility for accidents that may occur
    C. improve the employees' skills
    D. acquaint employees with their duties and responsibilities

17._____

18. If, when you are using an extension light with a long cord, the light should go out unexpectedly, you should FIRST
    A. inspect the cord for a broken wire
    B. replace the bulb with a new one
    C. check the fuses in the supply circuit
    D. check if the plug is still in the outlet

18._____

19. The MOST common danger in working around rotating machinery is from
    A. the suction effect created
    B. static electricity
    C. flying particles
    D. catching clothing on the moving parts

19._____

20. Acetylene is commonly used
    A. in cutting steel with a torch
    B. as a rust remover
    C. for extinguishing fires
    D. as a solvent for cleaning instruments

20._____

21. In drilling a hole which is to be tapped for a 3/8" screw, the twist drill size is
    A. 1/8"   B. 5/16"   C. 3/8"   D. 7/16"

21._____

22. The material which is an alloy is
    A. aluminum   B. tin   C. zinc   D. bronze

22._____

23. Cold chisels with "mushroomed" heads are repaired by
    A. cutting with hacksaw   B. turning
    C. grinding   D. hammering

23._____

24. In a first aid kit, you would NOT expect to find
    A. bandages   B. absorbent cotton
    C. splints for a broken leg   D. band-aids

24._____

25. In treating injuries it is MOST important that any bandages used be
    A. clean   B. damp   C. large   D. waterproof

25._____

KEY (CORRECT ANSWERS)

1. B	11. A	21. B
2. A	12. B	22. D
3. A	13. C	23. C
4. B	14. A	24. C
5. A	15. C	25. A
6. A	16. D	
7. C	17. D	
8. D	18. D	
9. C	19. D	
10. D	20. A	

TEST 2

DIRECTIONS: Each question or incomplete statement is followed by several suggested answers or completions. Select the one that BEST answers the question or completes the statement. *PRINT THE LETTER OF THE CORRECT ANSWER IN THE SPACE AT THE RIGHT.*

Questions 1-9 refer to the figures below:

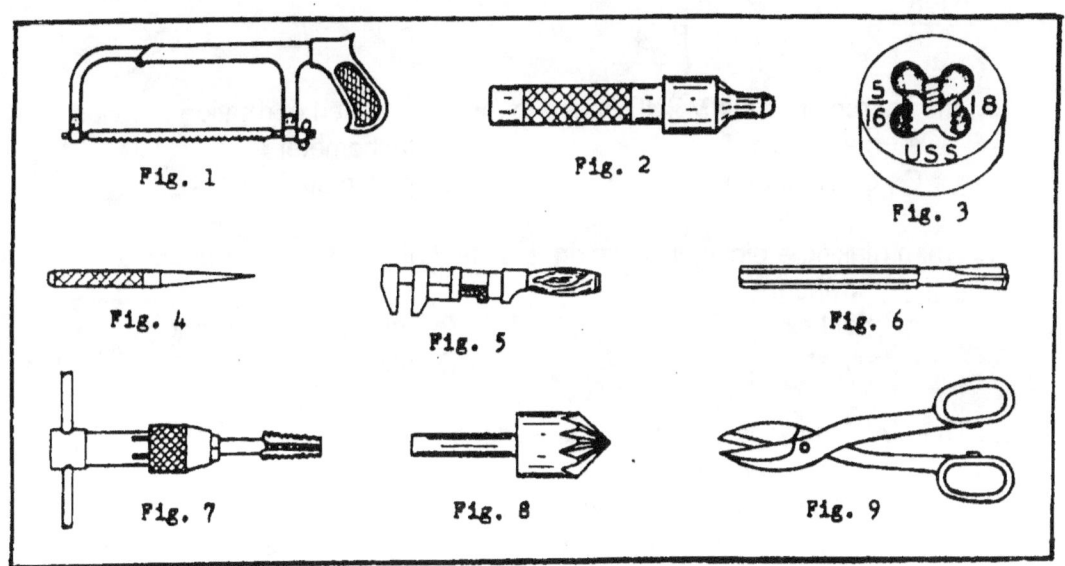

1. To thread a rod the tool to use is that shown in figure   1._____
   A. 3   B. 6   C. 7   D. 8

2. The tool shown in figure 9 ordinarily would NOT be used to cut a   2._____
   A. sheet of aluminum   B. sheet of copper
   C. sheet of paper   D. tin plate

3. In figure 5 there is shown a(n) _____ wrench.   3._____
   A. monkey   B. stillson   C. strap   D. open-end

4. The PROPER use for the tool shown in figure 4 would be as a   4._____
   A. center punch   B. drift pin
   C. pick   D. scriber

5. The tool shown in figure 7 is used in   5._____
   A. broaching   B. drilling   C. tapping   D. reaming

6. The tool shown in figure 8 is used in   6._____
   A. reaming   B. countersinking
   C. counterboring   D. cutting concrete

5

2 (#2)

7. A star drill is shown in figure 7._____
   A. 2   B. 6   C. 7   D. 8

8. The number "18" shown on the tool of figure 3 indicates 8._____
   A. type of thread   B. size of opening
   C. depth of opening   D. threads per inch

9. The tool to use to properly flare one end of copper tubing is shown in figure 9._____
   A. 2   B. 4   C. 6   D. 8

10. The instrument COMMONLY used to measure speed of rotation is called a 10._____
    A. manometer   B. tachometer
    C. chronometer   D. planimeter

11. When making a piping installation, the steel pipe is BEST turned by a _____ wrench. 11._____
    A. monkey   B. adjustable open-end
    C. alligator   D. stillson

12. The MAIN purpose of periodic inspections and tests made on equipment which is in constant use is to 12._____
    A. familiarize the operating men with the equipment
    B. keep the maintenance men busy during otherwise slack periods
    C. discover minor faults before they develop into serious breakdowns
    D. encourage the men to take better care of the equipment

13. A large oil storage tank has several manholes for easy access to the interior for periodic cleaning. You would NOT expect any of the manhole cover plates to be fastened to the tank by means of 13._____
    A. hinges and bolts   B. rivets
    C. studs and nuts   D. swing bolts and nuts

14. Compound used on threaded pipe joints should be applied on 14._____
    A. the piece that is threaded on the outside
    B. the joint edge after tightening
    C. both threaded pieces
    D. the piece that is threaded on the inside

15. When installed on moving machinery or shafting, set screws are often recessed so that no part of the screw sticks up above the surface MAINLY for 15._____
    A. strength   B. appearance   C. balance   D. safety

16. When using a portable extension cord and lamp, an important safety precaution to take is to make sure that the cord
    A. is not too long
    B. does not kink
    C. does not create a tripping hazard
    D. does not lie in dirt

17. If a machine screw does NOT turn easily with the screwdriver you are using, you should try one with a
    A. sharper tip
    B. wider tip
    C. longer blade
    D. thicker handle

18. The presence of lubricating oil on shop floors is
    A. good because it lays the dust
    B. bad because it causes accidents
    C. good because it absorbs moisture and prevents dampness
    D. bad because it injures cement floors

19. The fastening at the points marked "X" in the steel drum shown below is MOST commonly done with

    A. rivets
    B. machine screws
    C. lag screws
    D. bolts

20. A piece is to be cut out of the angle iron in order to make the right angle bracket shown. Angle "X" should be _____ degrees.

    A. 30   B. 45   C. 60   D. 90

21. A screwed fitting bypass is shown without valves. In making up this   21._____
    bypass the gap would be occupied by a standard

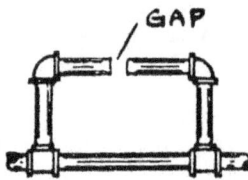

    A. coupling   B. expansion joint
    C. close nipple   D. union

22. The 2" pipe run shown has a pitch of 1/4" per foot. The total rise in 25' is   22._____

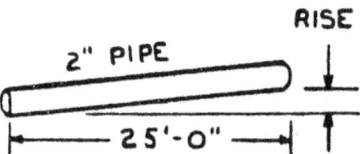

    A. 4 1/4"   B. 5 1/4"   C. 6 1/4"   D. 8 1/4"

23. The pitch (or distance between centers) of the evenly spaced tubes is   23._____

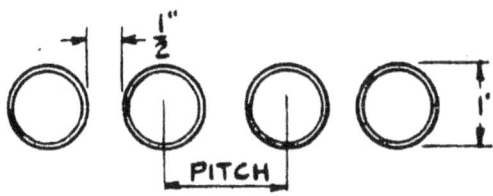

    A. 2 1/2"   B. 1 1/2"   C. 1"   D/ 3/4"

24. The flange bolts should be pulled up with a pair of   24._____

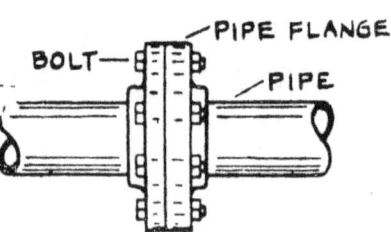

    A. monkey wrenches   B. stillson wrenches
    C. strap wrenches   D. open-end wrenches

5 (#2)

25. The distance "X" between the centers of the two end holes is   25._____

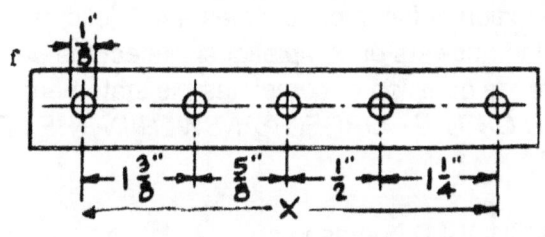

A. 3 3/4"   B. 3 1/2"   C. 3"   D. 2 3/4"

KEY (CORRECT ANSWERS)

1. A	11. D	21. D
2. C	12. C	22. C
3. A	13. B	23. B
4. D	14. A	24. D
5. C	15. D	25. A
6. B	16. C	
7. B	17. D	
8. D	18. B	
9. A	19. A	
10. B	20. D	

TEST 3

DIRECTIONS: Each question or incomplete statement is followed by several suggested answers or completions. Select the one that BEST answers the question or completes the statement. *PRINT THE LETTER OF THE CORRECT ANSWER IN THE SPACE AT THE RIGHT.*

1. Accident reports SHOULD be based on
 A. conclusions B. facts C. opinions D. theories

2. The jaws of a vise close 3/16 of an inch for each turn of the screw. If the vise is open 6 inches, the number of turns required to close the jaw is
 A. 8 B. 16 C. 32 D. 64

3. Bolts are usually designated by
 A. diameter and length
 B. weight and diameter
 C. number per pound
 D. weight of each

4. To polish a steel rod, the BEST material to use would be
 A. sand paper
 B. emery cloth
 C. terry cloth
 D. crocus cloth

5. Alcohol is COMMONLY used as a(n)
 A. anti-freeze
 B. lubricant
 C. paint thinner
 D. rust remover

6. On a piece of round stock turning in a lathe it is POOR practice to use a file
 A. at all
 B. without a handle
 C. that has sharp teeth
 D. when the lathe is turning fast

7. Holes are usually countersunk for
 A. carriage bolts
 B. lag screws
 C. flat head screws
 D. square nuts

8. If the inside diameter of a pipe is 3/8 of an inch and the wall thickness is .091 inches, the outside diameter of the pipe is _____ inches.
 A. .193 B. .284 C. .466 D. .557

9. A tapered thread is used on a water pipe. The advantage of using a tapered thread is that
 A. it is easier to cut
 B. it helps make a tight joint
 C. no joint compound needs to be used
 D. it reduces the weight of the piping

10. The teeth of a hacksaw are generally set so as to make a cut wider than the saw blade. This is done MAINLY to
    A. permit easy movement of the blade
    B. strengthen the teeth
    C. prevent dulling the blade
    D. cool the blade

10._____

11. A hole has been drilled in a piece of metal and it is necessary to enlarge it by 0.010 of an inch to an exact size. The PROPER tool to use is a
    A. countersink   B. drill
    C. reamer   D. rat-tail file

11._____

Questions 12 through 23 refer to the figures shown below:

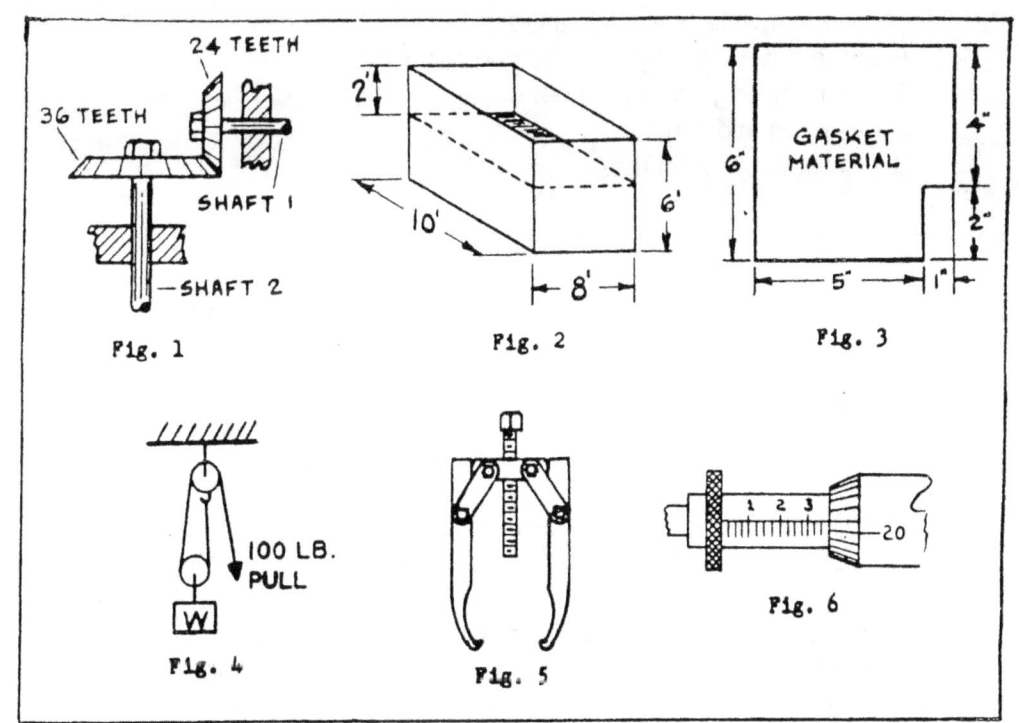

12. In figure 1 are shown two _____ gears.
    A. spur   B. herringbone   C. worm   D. bevel

12._____

13. In figure 1, when shaft 2 revolves at 150 rpm, shaft 1 revolves at ___ rpm.
    A. 225   B. 150   C. 100   D. 60

13._____

14. The TOTAL capacity of the partly filled tank in figure 2, in cubic feet, is
    A. 160   B. 240   C. 320   D. 480

14._____

15. The tank in figure 2, as shown, is _____ full.
    A. 1/3   B. 1/2   C. 2/3   D. 3/4

15._____

16. The diameter of the LARGEST circular gasket that may be cut from the gasket material in figure 3 is
    A. 2"   B. 4"   C. 5"   D. 6"

17. The area in square inches of the gasket material in figure 3 is
    A. 28   B. 32   C. 34   D. 36

18. The perimeter in inches of the gasket material in figure 3 is
    A. 18   B. 24   C. 30   D. 36

19. In figure 4 the MAXIMUM weight "W" that can be lifted as shown with a pull of 100 pounds is _____ lbs.
    A. 50   B. 100   C. 200   D. 300

20. The device shown in figure 5 is used
    A. to remove a pulley from the end of a shaft
    B. for punching holes in sheet metal
    C. as a jog in drilling
    D. to extract broken taps

21. In figure 5, to turn the bolt you would NOT use a(n) _____ wrench.
    A. stillson
    B. monkey
    C. box
    D. adjustable open-end

22. In figure 6 there is shown a
    A. vernier caliper
    B. snap gauge
    C. micrometer caliper
    D. thread gauge

23. The reading on the instrument shown in figure 6 is
    A. 0.322"   B. 0.361"   C. 0.369"   D. 0.371"

24. If it is necessary for you to make some adjustment with your hands under a piece of heavy equipment, while a fellow worker lifts up and holds one end of it by means of a pinch bar, one important precaution you should take is to
    A. insert a temporary block to support the piece
    B. watch the bar to be ready if it slips
    C. wear gloves
    D. work as fast as possible

25. If a measurement scaled from a drawing is one inch, and the scale of the drawing is 1/4 inch to the foot, then the one-inch measurement would represent an actual length of
    A. 4 feet   B. 2 feet   C. 1/4 of a foot   D. 4 inches

KEY (CORRECT ANSWERS)

1. B	11. C	21. A
2. C	12. D	22. C
3. A	13. A	23. C
4. D	14. D	24. A
5. A	15. C	25. A
6. B	16. C	
7. C	17. C	
8. D	18. B	
9. B	19. C	
10. A	20. A	

TEST 4

DIRECTIONS: Each question or incomplete statement is followed by several suggested answers or completions. Select the one that BEST answers the question or completes the statement. *PRINT THE LETTER OF THE CORRECT ANSWER IN THE SPACE AT THE RIGHT.*

1. A circular disc is divided into 18 equal segments, each segment will have an angular section of
    A. 10°   B. 15°   C. 20°   D. 24°

    1._____

2. A lathe collar is BASICALLY a
    A. drill
    B. chuck
    C. mandrel
    D. knurling tool

    2._____

3. Babbitt hammers are used in machine shops PRINCIPALLY to
    A. protect workmen from flying chips
    B. prevent sparks
    C. prevent marring the work
    D. reduce noise

    3._____

4. A protractor is an instrument for measuring
    A. angles
    B. area
    C. the depth of drilled holes
    D. the thickness of sheet metal

    4._____

5. A ladder which is painted is a safety hazard MAINLY because the paint
    A. is slippery after drying
    B. may conceal weak spots in the rails and rungs
    C. causes the wood to crack more quickly
    D. peels and the wood starts to decay

    5._____

6. The MAIN reason for imbedding steel rods in concrete is to
    A. prevent the rods from rusting
    B. decrease the density of the concrete
    C. increase the strength of the concrete
    D. increase the weight of the concrete

    6._____

7. A department rule prohibits indulgence in intoxicating liquor, or being under its influence, while on duty. This rule is rigidly enforced in order to
    A. prevent an employee from endangering himself or others
    B. help promote temperance
    C. enable an employee to save money
    D. eliminate absenteeism

    7._____

8. Standard forms frequently call for entries on them to be printed. The MAIN reason for this practice is that printing, as compared to writing, is generally
   A. more compact
   B. more legal
   C. more legible
   D. easier to do

9. The instrument COMMONLY used to measure the diameter of a piece of work in a lathe is a
   A. micrometer caliper
   B. pair of outside calipers
   C. vernier caliper
   D. pair of dividers

10. The MOST important reason for roping off the work area when repairs are made is to
    A. prevent delays to the public
    B. protect the repair crew
    C. prevent distraction of the crew by the public
    D. protect the public

11. Copper liners are often put on the jaws of a vise to
    A. protect the jaws of the vise
    B. protect the work
    C. decrease noise
    D. grip the work tighter

12. If a coworker is in contact with a high-voltage circuit, the FIRST action taken should be to
    A. call a doctor
    B. use a resuscitation method on him
    C. call the foreman
    D. cut off power

13. The "gauge" of sheet metal indicates the sheet's
    A. width   B. thickness   C. length   D. area

14. When used in reference to pipe, the abbreviations I.D. and O.D. refer to the pipe
    A. density   B. diameters   C. length   D. weight

15. The BEST immediate first aid for a scraped knee is to
    A. apply plain Vaseline
    B. apply an ice pack
    C. apply heat
    D. wash it with soap and water

16. Of the sizes of sandpaper given, the FINEST is
    A. 1/2   B. 0   C. 00   D. 000

17. Powdered graphite is a good
    A. abrasive   B. adhesive   C. insulator   D. lubricant

18. A particular casting will be LIGHTEST in weight if made of 18._____
    A. cast iron   B. aluminum   C. brass   D. steel

19. To prevent an ordinary steel nut from working loose under vibration, the 19._____
BEST device to use is a
    A. cotton pin   B. drop of solder
    C. fibre washer   D. lock washer

20. The head of a small rivet is readily formed with a 20._____
    A. ball peen hammer   B. claw hammer
    C. center punch   D. nail set

21. The machine used to bend sheet metal is called a 21._____
    A. brake   B. miller   C. planer   D. router

22. The word "plan" when used on a blueprint indicates 22._____
    A. a side elevation view   B. a top view
    C. a front elevation view   D. the order of assembly

23. Drilling must be done with special care when using any one of the very 23._____
small size twist drills because the
    A. drill speed may be too fast
    B. the drill is apt to break
    C. cut material will clog the drill
    D. drill may overheat

24. A parting tool is USUALLY used for work in a 24._____
    A. planer   B. milling machine
    C. lathe   D. shaper

25. Diagonal pliers are PROPERLY used to 25._____
    A. cut pipe   B. flatten steel tubing
    C. turn hexagonal nuts   D. cut wire

KEY (CORRECT ANSWERS)

1. C	11. B	21. A
2. B	12. D	22. B
3. C	13. B	23. B
4. A	14. B	24. C
5. B	15. D	25. D
6. C	16. D	
7. A	17. D	
8. C	18. B	
9. B	19. D	
10. D	20. A	

EXAMINATION SECTION

TEST 1

DIRECTIONS: Each question or incomplete statement is followed by several suggested answers or completions. Select the one that BEST answers the question or completes the statement. *PRINT THE LETTER OF THE CORRECT ANSWER IN THE SPACE AT THE RIGHT.*

1. A drill gauge is used for measuring drill
   A. length   B. diameter   C. hardness   D. pitch

   1._____

2. The wrench which is LEAST likely to slip off a nut of standard size is a(n)
   A. "S" wrench   B. box wrench
   C. monkey wrench   D. adjustable open-end wrench

   2._____

3. Wing nuts are especially useful when
   A. the nut is to be removed frequently
   B. space is limited
   C. vibration effects must be counteracted
   D. the nut is never to be removed

   3._____

4. Gauge blocks are used for checking the accuracy of
   A. micrometers   B. levels
   C. dividers   D. spring calipers

   4._____

5. The proper shop machine to use in order to plane flat steel stock is a
   A. shaper   B. lathe
   C. brake   D. boring mill

   5._____

6. On a lathe, a face-plate is sometimes used instead of a
   A. compound rest   B. tool post
   C. chuck   D. saddle

   6._____

7. Of the following, it would be MOST difficult to hand file
   A. brass   B. stainless steel
   C. copper   D. lead

   7._____

8. A screw which USUALLY has a square head is a _____ screw.
   A. lag   B. Phillips head
   C. fillister head D. thumb

   8._____

9. Of the following, the BEST precaution to take when removing a broken tap by using a hammer and punch is to
   A. wear gloves   B. wear goggles
   C. use a soft hammer D. lubricate the punch

   9._____

19

10. Speed and feed CANNOT be varied independently of each other when
    A. drilling   B. tapping   C. boring   D. reaming

11. Of the following, the dimension which calls for the HIGHEST accuracy and provides for the LEAST tolerance is
    A. 3.05" ± .01"
    B. 3.020" ± .005"
    C. 3.010" ± .002"
    D. 3.025"

12. An oilstone would be LEAST likely used to sharpen a
    A. scraper   B. chisel   C. knife   D. saw

13. It would be POOR practice to use a flat cold chisel to
    A. cut thin sheet metal
    B. cut a semi-circular groove in a steel block
    C. split a nut
    D. cut a rivet

14. A hole drilled in a shaft would PROBABLY be reamed to fit a
    A. cotter pin
    B. cap screw
    C. taper pin
    D. carriage bolt

15. A soft-face hammer would NOT have a pounding surface made of
    A. copper   B. babbitt   C. lead   D. steel

16. V-blocks are especially useful for holding
    A. square pieces
    B. circular bars
    C. flat plates
    D. hexagonal pieces

Questions 17 through 24 are based on the following passage:

SUBWAY CAR AIR COMPRESSOR SYSTEM

A two-stage, motor-driven air compressor having a large low-pressure cylinder and a smaller high-pressure cylinder is used. The low-pressure cylinder, fitted with an air intake filter, performs the first stage of compression and discharges through an intercooler into the high-pressure cylinder where the second stage of compression is performed. An unloader valve insures that compression does not begin until the motor has reached its full speed. An aftercooler is located between the compressor discharge and compressor reservoir. An automatic drain valve located on the compressor reservoir automatically discharges precipitated moisture from the reservoir whenever the compressor governor functions to cur in power or shut off power to the compressor motor. The governor operates to stop the compressor when the reservoir air pressure reaches 140 lbs. and to start the compressor when the reservoir air pressure drops to 125 lbs. A safety valve set at 150 lbs. is connected to the compressor reservoir.

17. The number of air-cooling devices provided in the compressor system is   17._____
    A. 1   B. 2   C. 3   D. 4

18. When the motor is starting up, it is protected by the   18._____
    A. safety valve   B. governor
    C. drain valve   D. unloader valve

19. The intake filter is MOST likely designed to screen out   19._____
    A. dirt   B. water   C. oil   D. heat

20. The air pressure is LOWEST in the   20._____
    A. small cylinder   B. large cylinder
    C. compressor reservoir   D. aftercooler

21. The automatic drain valve is triggered by the   21._____
    A. governor   B. unloader valve
    C. safety valve   D. intercooler

22. The motor should stop running when the reservoir air pressure reaches _____ pounds.   22._____
    A. 125   B. 130   C. 135   D. 140

23. Water automatically drains from the   23._____
    A. low pressure cylinder   B. high-pressure cylinder
    C. air reservoir   D. intercooler

24. Compression begins with the motor   24._____
    A. off   B. at low speed
    C. at intermediate speed   D. at full speed

25. A steel rod having a diameter of 2-1/8 inches is to be discarded when worn more than .005 inches. The MINIMUM diameter permissible for this rod is   25._____
    A. 2.125"   B. 2.120"   C. 2.075"   D. 1.625"

KEY (CORRECT ANSWERS)

1. B	11. C	21. A
2. B	12. D	22. D
3. A	13. B	23. C
4. A	14. C	24. D
5. A	15. D	25. B
6. C	16. B	
7. B	17. B	
8. A	18. D	
9. B	19. A	
10. B	20. B	

TEST 2

DIRECTIONS: Each question or incomplete statement is followed by several suggested answers or completions. Select the one that BEST answers the question or completes the statement. *PRINT THE LETTER OF THE CORRECT ANSWER IN THE SPACE AT THE RIGHT.*

1. Incorrect use of a machinist's hammer frequently results in uneven face wear. To properly recondition the face of the hammer, it would be BEST to use a
    A. milling machine
    B. shaper
    C. grinder
    D. file

    1._____

2. A stubby screwdriver is especially designed for turning screws
    A. having a damaged screw slot
    B. which are jammed tight
    C. inaccessible to a longer screwdriver
    D. with stripped threads

    2._____

3. Allen-type wrenches are USUALLY L-shaped. This shape
    A. is only for distinguishing it from other wrenches
    B. is used to make the wrench sturdier
    C. permits a higher leverage with the short end inserted in a screw to be tightened
    D. permits a higher leverage with the long end inserted in a screw to be tightened

    3._____

4. On a lathe, when a fixed cut is made at right angles to the axis of the work, the operation is known as
    A. straight turning
    B. taper cutting
    C. boring
    D. reaming

    4._____

5. The MOST important reason for dipping a chisel into cold water when it is being ground is to
    A. provide lubrication for the grinding process
    B. keep the chisel clean
    C. preserve the temper of the chisel
    D. reduce the wear on the grinding wheel

    5._____

6. To determine the taper per inch of a piece of work by using a steel scale, the number of dimensions to be measured if the piece is a cone is a MINIMUM of
    A. one   B. two   C. three   D. four

    6._____

23

2 (#2)

7. A drilled hole is spotfaced 7._____
   A. only if it is to be threaded
   B. to provide a smooth seat for a nut or cap screw head
   C. to bring the hole diameter to exact dimensions
   D. to strengthen the material around the hole

8. Open-end wrenches with small openings are generally made shorter in overall length than open-end wrenches with larger openings. The MOST important reason for this is to 8._____
   A. provide compactness
   B. save material
   C. provide correct leverage
   D. prevent cracking of the wrench

9. A tool used to remove taper shank drills from a drilling machine spindle is known as a 9._____
   A. drift
   B. dinking punch
   C. pin punch
   D. center punch

Questions 10 through 17 refer to the figures shown below:

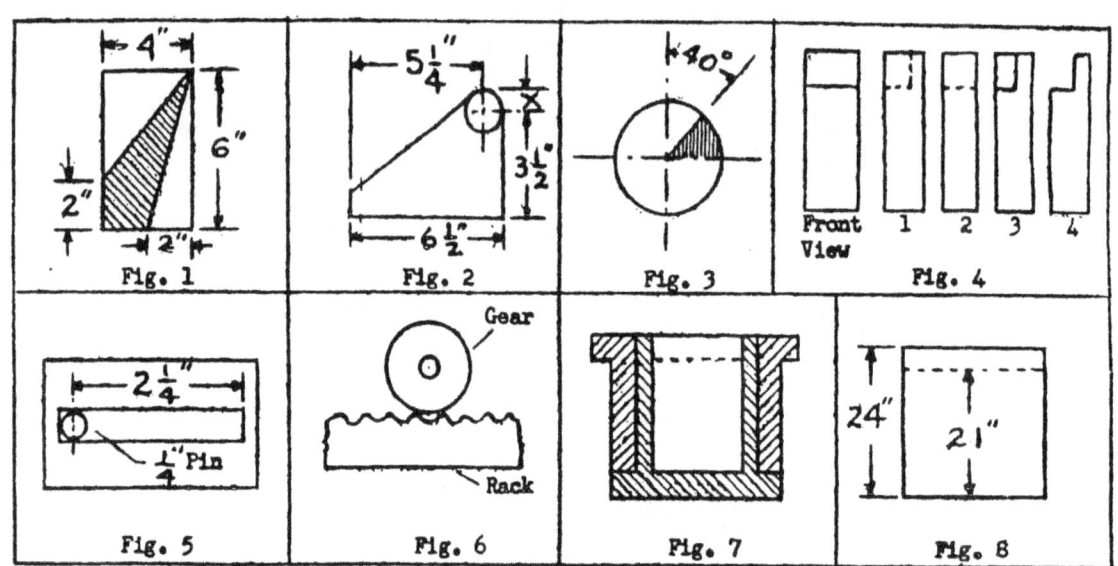

10. In figure 1, the area in square inches of the shaded portion of the rectangle is 10._____
    A. 28   B. 24   C. 14   D. 10

11. In figure 2, dimension "X" is 11._____
    A. 1.25"   B. 1.75"   C. 2"   D. 2.5"

12. Figure 3 shows a shaded sector on a circular metal sheet. The MAXIMUM number of such sectors which can be cut from the sheet is 12._____
    A. 7   B. 8   C. 9   D. 10

13. Figure 4 shows a front view of a steel piece. The correct side view is number
    A. 1   B. 2   C. 3   D. 4

    13._____

14. Figure 5 shows a circular pin which slides horizontally in a slotted rigid steel block. The MAXIMUM distance the pin can move, going from left to right, is
    A. 2 1/2"   B. 2 3/8"   C. 2 1/8"   D. 2"

    14._____

15. In figure 6, a gear with 30 teeth is turned by a gear rack having 20 teeth per inch. If the rack moves 3/4" horizontally, the gear will revolve
    A. 1/2 turn   B. 2/3 of a turn
    C. 1 1/2 turns   D. 2 turns

    15._____

16. In figure 7 is a cross-section of an assembly. The number of separate pieces is
    A. 1   B. 2   C. 3   D. 4

    16._____

17. Figure 8 shows a water tank having a total capacity of 120 gallons, which is partially filled. If 40 gallons are drained, the new water level will be _____ high.
    A. 16"   B. 13"   C. 10"   D. 8"

    17._____

18. A measuring rule used in special cases is a hooked scale. This type of scale would be MOST useful in cases where
    A. it is difficult to see if the edge of the rule is even with the edge from which the measurement is to be made
    B. the depth of a blind hole is to be measured
    C. the inside diameter of a hole is to be measured
    D. the circumference of a rod is to be measured

    18._____

19. A machine shop procedure is to rub a thin application of prussian blue on a surface plate and then rub the piece of work being tested on the plate. This procedure is MOST likely to be used to check a steel block which has been
    A. scraped   B. drilled   C. hacksawed   D. reamed

    19._____

20. Rubber tubing deteriorates MOST rapidly when in contact with
    A. water   B. air   C. oil   D. soap suds

    20._____

21. Ordinarily when using a file, pressure is applied on the forward stroke only. One exception to this rule is when filing
    A. lead   B. steel   C. cast iron   D. nickel

    21._____

22. The PROPER file to use for enlarging a hole would be a _____ file.
    A. flat   B. rat-tail   C. square   D. mill

    22._____

23. The diameter of a hole required to be 3.254" should be checked with   23._____
    A. an inside vernier caliper   B. dividers and a steel scale
    C. calipers and a steel scale   D. a micrometer depth gauge

24. When using a hacksaw, it is GOOD practice to   24._____
    A. tighten the blade in the frame by using pliers on the wing nut
    B. use heavy pressure on both the forward and return strokes
    C. slow the speed of cutting when the piece is almost cut through
    D. use very short, rapid strokes

25. With the standard measuring micrometer, starting with a zero reading,   25._____
    three complete revolutions of the sleeve will give a reading of
        A. 0.75"   B. 0.06"   C. 0.03"   D. 0.003"

KEY (CORRECT ANSWERS)

1. C	11. A	21. A
2. C	12. A	22. B
3. C	13. D	23. A
4. A	14. C	24. C
5. C	15. A	25. A
6. B	16. B	
7. B	17. B	
8. C	18. A	
9. A	19. A	
10. D	20. C	

TEST 3

DIRECTIONS: Each question or incomplete statement is followed by several suggested answers or completions. Select the one that BEST answers the question or completes the statement. *PRINT THE LETTER OF THE CORRECT ANSWER IN THE SPACE AT THE RIGHT.*

1. A NO-GO ring gauge fits loosely over a circular rod which is being checked. This would mean that the
    A. rod is satisfactory
    B. rod must be scrapped
    C. diameter of the rod must be reduced
    D. rod is too long

    1._____

2. A screwdriver bit and brace has an advantage over an ordinary screwdriver MAINLY because
    A. more leverage can be applied to tighten a screw
    B. the screwdriver bit cannot slip in a screw slot
    C. fewer turns are required to tighten a screw
    D. the bit is shorter than a screwdriver blade

    2._____

3. The PROPER way to clean a file which has been used on soft material is to use a
    A. piece of emery cloth   B. file card
    C. sharp scriber   D. bench brush

    3._____

4. When hand reamers are used the amount of metal to be removed is in the range of _____ of an inch.
    A. millionths   B. thousandths   C. hundredths   D. tens

    4._____

5. If a drill makes a hole larger than its diameter, a LIKELY cause would be
    A. too low a drill speed
    B. too sharp a drill
    C. that the drill has been ground out of center
    D. that the drill has cutting edges of equal length

    5._____

6. A counterbored hole is designed to take a(n) _____ screw.
    A. fillister head   B. flat head
    C. oval head   D. Phillips head

    6._____

7. A slight coating of rust on small tools is BEST removed by
    A. applying a heavy coat of Vaseline
    B. scraping with a sharp knife
    C. rubbing with kerosene and fine steel wool
    D. rubbing with a dry cloth

    7._____

8. If a coworker becomes caught in a running machine, the FIRST thing to do is to
    A. try to pull him out
    B. call the foreman
    C. call the shop physician
    D. shut the power off the machine

9. From a safety standpoint, the LEAST desirable time to wear gloves is when
    A. running a lathe
    B. carrying castings
    C. lifting heavy materials with a chain hoist
    D. handling hot objects

10. Before taking apart a mechanical assembly, one or more sets of center punch marks are made on the assembly. This is GENERALLY done in order to
    A. show the parts are new
    B. test the hardness of the metal
    C. make accurate reassembly easier
    D. facilitate disassembly

11. Galvanizing is a process used on sheet metal to
    A. increase its tensile strength
    B. make it rust-resistant
    C. soften it for drilling
    D. prepare it for welding

12. The MOST important reason for keeping a cold chisel free from oil or grease is to
    A. make it cut better
    B. avoid oil splattering from the blows
    C. prevent fire hazard when the tool heats up
    D. prevent the hammer from glancing off the chisel head

13. Cotter pins are MOST generally used with
    A. acorn nuts   B. castellated nuts
    C. knurled nuts   D. wing nuts

Questions 14 through 21 refer to the figures shown below:

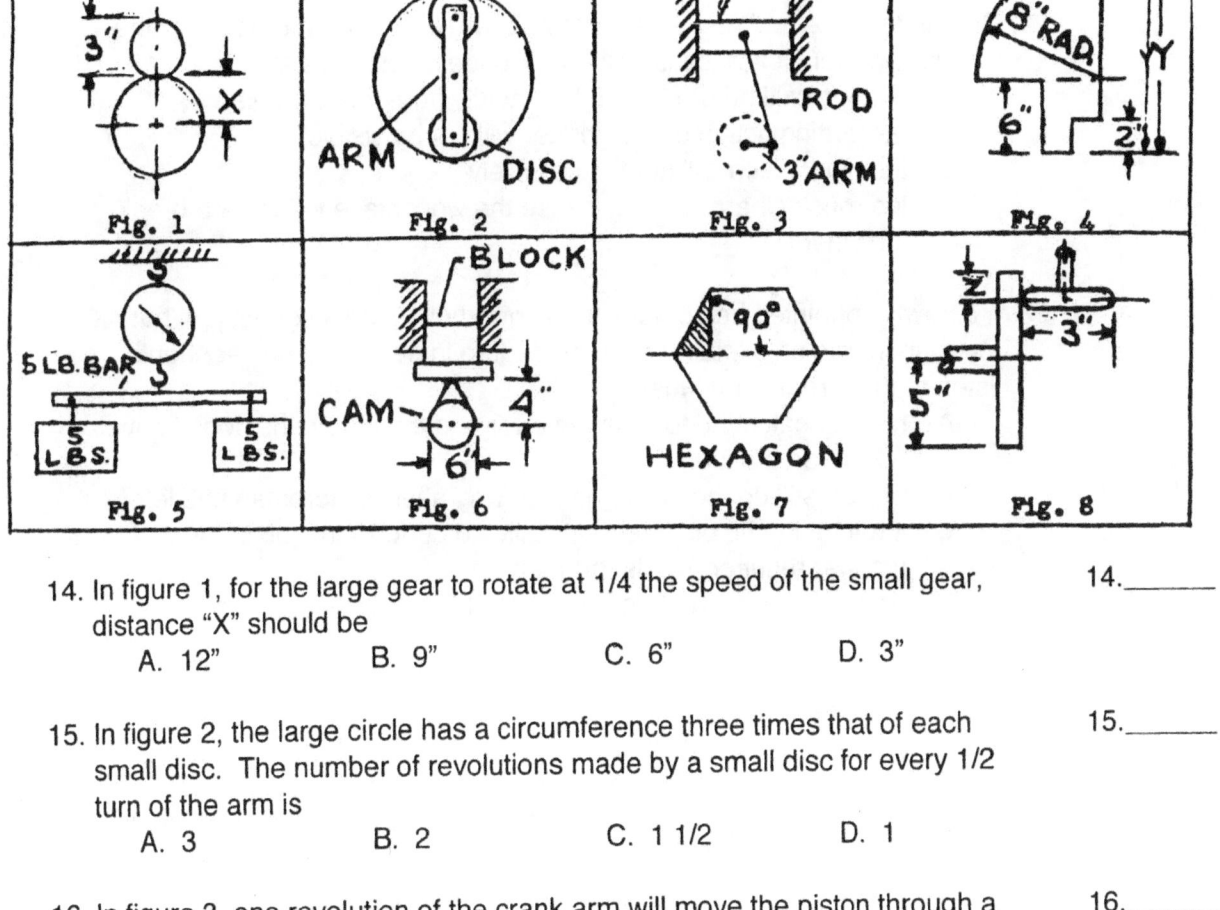

14. In figure 1, for the large gear to rotate at 1/4 the speed of the small gear, distance "X" should be
    A. 12" B. 9" C. 6" D. 3"

15. In figure 2, the large circle has a circumference three times that of each small disc. The number of revolutions made by a small disc for every 1/2 turn of the arm is
    A. 3 B. 2 C. 1 1/2 D. 1

16. In figure 3, one revolution of the crank arm will move the piston through a TOTAL distance of
    A. 3" B. 6" C. 9" D. 12"

17. In figure 4, the distance "Y" is
    A. 10" B. 12" C. 14" D. 16"

18. In figure 5, which shows a balanced bar, the weighing scale will read approximately _____ pounds.
    A. zero B. 5 C. 10 D. 15

19. In figure 6, rotation of the cam will permit the block to drop a MAXIMUM of
    A. 1" B. 4" C. 6" D. 7"

20. In figure 7, the total area of the hexagon will be found by multiplying the area of the shaded segment by
    A. 14 B. 12 C. 10 D. 8

21. In figure 8, both wheels will turn at the same speed when "Z" is
    A. 1.5"   B. 2"   C. 3"   D. 3.5"

22. On grinders, the tool rest is generally about 1/8 inch from the face of the wheel. Greater clearance is USUALLY undesirable because
    A. material will be ground off too rapidly from the work piece
    B. the cutting action of the grinder will not be visible
    C. the work piece will heat excessively
    D. too much clearance may cause the work piece to jam and break the wheel

23. If a newly appointed helper feels he knows how to do a certain job, but his foreman insists on explaining the procedure in detail, the helper should listen to the foreman because
    A. he may catch the foreman in error and thus prove he does know how to do the job
    B. he can still do the job in his own way after the foreman has left
    C. it will be the helper's responsibility to perform the job in the manner required by his foreman
    D. he must humor the foreman, even if the foreman is wrong

24. When using a hand file to finish a piece of work held between lathe centers, it is generally BEST to
    A. do the finishing operation without running the lathe
    B. use only one hand to hold and guide the file
    C. hold the handle of the file in one hand and use the other hand to help guide the file
    D. use a file that has no handle

25. A flat steel bar two feet long, which is given a 90° twist at the midpoint, will
    A. increase in overall length
    B. still be exactly two feet long from end to end
    C. be better able to resist a bending force
    D. be better able to resist a tension force

KEY (CORRECT ANSWERS)

1. B	11. B	21. D
2. A	12. D	22. D
3. B	13. B	23. C
4. B	14. C	24. C
5. C	15. C	25. C
6. A	16. D	
7. C	17. C	
8. D	18. D	
9. A	19. A	
10. C	20. B	

TEST 4

DIRECTIONS: Each question or incomplete statement is followed by several suggested answers or completions. Select the one that BEST answers the question or completes the statement. *PRINT THE LETTER OF THE CORRECT ANSWER IN THE SPACE AT THE RIGHT.*

1. The dimension "6-inch" when used in connection with a screwdriver refers to the length of the
   A. handle
   B. ferrule
   C. screwdriver from end to end
   D. blade

2. When tapping a drilled hole, the tap diameter
   A. is greater than the hole diameter
   B. is smaller than the hole diameter
   C. is exactly equal to the hole diameter
   D. depends on the depth of the hole

3. A serious safety hazard occurs when a
   A. soft hammer is used to strike a hardened steel surface
   B. hardened steel hammer is used to strike a soft iron surface
   C. soft hammer is used to strike a soft iron surface
   D. hardened steel hammer is used to strike a hardened steel surface

4. After a piece of work has been set into a lathe for machining, it is good practice to revolve the work one complete revolution by hand, before running the lathe with power on. The MAIN reason for doing this is to
   A. make certain the lathe gears are not overloaded
   B. make certain the lathe is running true
   C. see there is ample clearance between work, dog, chuck and carriage
   D. get the feel of the work

5. A non-adjustable wrench which will accommodate different size nuts is a(n) _____ wrench.
   A. stillson
   B. monkey
   C. chain
   D. alligator

6. On your first day on the job as a helper, you are assigned to work with a maintainer. During the course of the work, you realize that the maintainer is about to violate a basic safety rule. In this case, the BEST thing for you to do is
   A. say nothing until he actually violates the safety rule and then call it to his attention
   B. say nothing, but later report this action to the foreman
   C. walk away from him so that you will not become involved
   D. immediately call it to his attention

7. The MAIN reason for using copper tips in soldering irons is because copper is
   A. a good electrical conductor
   B. a good heat conductor
   C. has a low melting point
   D. very soft

8. The material discharged by a carbon dioxide fire extinguisher should NOT be handled because it
   A. is a poisonous liquid
   B. is highly volatile
   C. is valuable for re-use
   D. can cause a frostbite

9. In order to cast a number of duplicate parts, it is generally necessary to first make a mold from a
   A. template   B. fixture   C. pattern   D. jog

10. There are a few workers who are seemingly prone to accidents and who, regardless of their assigned job, have a higher accident rate than the average worker. If your coworker is known to be such an individual, the BEST course for you to pursue would be to
    A. warn him not to make mistakes
    B. provide him with a copy of all rules and regulations
    C. do most of the assigned work yourself
    D. personally check safety precautions on each job

11. In a large shop, helpers are expected to do their work in a definitely prescribed manner because
    A. good results are more certain with less supervision
    B. it insures discipline
    C. no other method would work
    D. it permits speed-up

12. A new helper is told by an experienced helper that he is not doing a particular job properly. The BEST reason for the new helper to give this advice due consideration is that the other helper
    A. has the authority to enforce his advice
    B. has more experience on the job
    C. will be resentful if his advice is not taken
    D. will not help the new man again if his advice is not taken

13. A nail set is a tool used for
    A. straightening bent nails
    B. cutting nails to specified size
    C. sinking a nail head in wood
    D. measuring nail size

14. It is important to make certain a ladle does not contain water before using it to scoop up molten solder since the water may
    A. cause serious personal injury
    B. prevent the solder from sticking
    C. cool the solder
    D. dilute the solder

15. The device used to locate the center of a hole to be drilled in the same position on a number of identical castings is called a(n)
    A. circular chaser
    B. guide pillar
    C. blanking tool
    D. jig

16. A new helper trying to complete a job on time finds that he is being delayed by a maintainer who keeps engaging him in conversation concerning sports activities. It would be BEST for the helper to
    A. complain about this to the man's foreman
    B. simply continue to work and turn his back on the man without answering him
    C. converse with the man so that he will not antagonize him and later explain why the job wasn't finished on time
    D. tell the man he has no time to talk since he must finish the job on time

17. It is NOT good practice to cut thin-walled copper tubing with an ordinary three-wheel pipe cutter because
    A. the tubing is likely to collapse
    B. too much time is required
    C. the tubing end must be reamed after cutting
    D. the cutters will be dulled

18. When grinding a weld smooth it is MOST important to avoid
    A. grinding too slowly
    B. overheating the surrounding metal
    C. grinding too much of the weld away
    D. grinding after the weld has cooled off

19. Cadmium plating is applied to iron brackets and hangers after the parts have been drilled. The reason for plating after drilling is
    A. the plating makes the metal too hard to drill
    B. to avoid the safety hazard in drilling cadmium plated materials
    C. to save plating material
    D. to protect the inside surfaces of the holes

20. A gouge is a carpenter's tool used for removing material by
    A. filing
    B. grinding
    C. drilling
    D. chiseling

21. To make certain two points separated by a vertical distance of 8 feet are in perfect vertical alignment, it would be BEST to use a(n)
    A. height gauge
    B. plumb bob
    C. surface gauge
    D. protractor

22. Steel helmets give workers the MOST protection from
    A. falling objects
    B. eye injuries
    C. fire
    D. electric shock

23. A claw hammer is PROPERLY used for
    A. driving a cold chisel
    B. driving nails
    C. setting rivets
    D. bending steel

24. When mounting and fastening enamel sign plates, care MUST be taken to prevent
    A. corrosion
    B. chipping
    C. electrolysis
    D. discoloration

25. Employees of the department are cautioned not to use water to extinguish fires caused by high voltage arcing. The MOST likely reason for this rule is that water
    A. would cause the fuses to blow in the electrical circuits
    B. will cause corrosion of sensitive electrical parts
    C. coming into contact with a hot electrical arc causes asphyxiating fumes to be generated
    D. may conduct the electrical current and create a shock hazard

KEY (CORRECT ANSWERS)

1. D	11. A	21. B
2. A	12. B	22. A
3. D	13. C	23. B
4. C	14. A	24. B
5. D	15. D	25. D
6. D	16. D	
7. B	17. A	
8. D	18. C	
9. C	19. D	
10. D	20. D	

EXAMINATION SECTION

TEST 1

DIRECTIONS: Each question or incomplete statement is followed by several suggested answers or completions. Select the one that BEST answers the question or completes the statement. *PRINT THE LETTER OF THE CORRECT ANSWER IN THE SPACE AT THE RIGHT.*

1. When installing a new abrasive wheel on a grinder, it is GOOD practice to
    A. force-fit the wheel on the spindle
    B. burnish the spindle to insure a snug fit
    C. tighten the spindle nut as tightly as possible and then back it off 1/2 a turn
    D. tighten the spindle nut just enough for the flanges to hold the wheel firmly

1._____

2. The points of a steel divide are BEST sharpened
    A. with a small hand oilstone moistened with light oil
    B. on a high-speed grinder
    C. with a half-round file
    D. on a lathe

2._____

3. To repair a machinist's steel chisel which has a mushroomed head, the PROPER procedure is to
    A. hacksaw the mushroomed head off
    B. countersink the mushroomed head
    C. soften the chisel and reshape the head on a lathe
    D. grind the head to its original shape and harden the chisel

3._____

4. Hand taps for making threads generally come in sets of three, respectively called taper, second and bottoming taps. When tapping a blind hole in a steel block, the
    A. taper tap is used last
    B. bottoming tap is used first
    C. second tap is never used
    D. bottoming tap is used to complete the thread at the bottom of the hole

4._____

5. The star drill is a multiple-pointed chisel used for drilling
    A. brass
    B. stone and concrete
    C. wood
    D. aluminum

5._____

6. Shop employees are required to promptly report when first-aid supplies are used. The MOST important reason for this is to
   A. figure the costs of these supplies
   B. prevent theft of these supplies
   C. make certain first-aid supplies are immediately replenished
   D. determine if the first aid was properly administered

7. Generally all scale, rust and grease are removed from materials before they are welded. This is MAINLY done in order to
   A. make the area to be welded clearly visible
   B. prevent the weld from cooling too rapidly
   C. reduce accident hazard
   D. reduce the amount of welding material required

8. One advantage of the ordinary closed-end flat wrench is that
   A. it provides a better hand grip than other wrenches
   B. it has no open jaws which tend to spread easily
   C. it is adjustable for various nut sizes
   D. the same wrench can be used for square and hexagon nuts

9. A tool which would NOT be used in an electric drill is a(n)
   A. twist drill
   B. reamer
   C. auger bit
   D. flat drill

10. When using a hacksaw, it would be POOR practice to
    A. relieve pressure on the backstroke
    B. saw more rapidly when the blade is almost through the cut
    C. saw close to the point where the work is clamped
    D. set the blade in the frame so that the forward stroke will be the cutting stroke

11. The BEST file to use for sharpening a rip saw is a(n)
    A. triangular file
    B. rasp
    C. round file
    D. square file

12. A soldering iron should be tinned
    A. before soldering
    B. when cold
    C. only when storing it
    D. only when soldering tin pieces

13. Ordinary solder is made of
    A. tin and brass
    B. lead and copper
    C. tin, lead and copper
    D. tin and lead

14. The purpose of the compound rest on a lathe is to 14._____
    A. support the cutting tool in its various positions
    B. hold the live center
    C. hold the dead center
    D. hold the necessary gears for obtaining the various spindle speeds

15. In order to cast a number of duplicate parts, it is GENERALLY necessary 15._____
    to FIRST make a mold from a(n)
    A. jig   B. template   C. pattern   D. fixture

16. A holding nut is USUALLY used with a(n) 16._____
    A. lag screw   B. self-tapping screw
    C. drive screw   D. stove bolt

17. The abrasive which is NOT commonly available in coarse quality is 17._____
    A. sandpaper   B. emery
    C. carborundum   D. crocus cloth

18. Spot welding is MOST commonly used to 18._____
    A. hold structural beams together
    B. fix long deep cracks in heavy castings
    C. fasten light metal sheets together
    D. make long watertight seams

19. A steel rod required to have an initial diameter of 3-1/8 inches is to be 19._____
    discarded when worn more than .005 inches. The MINIMUM diameter
    permissible for this steel rod is _____ inches.
    A. 3.145   B. 3.120   C. 3.065   D. 2.755

20. A mitre box is used for 20._____
    A. holding a saw at a fixed angle to the work
    B. storing sensitive measuring instruments
    C. setting the angle of the cutting tool on a lathe
    D. supporting heavy units

21. A taper on a piece of round stock is MOST usually made on a(n) 21._____
    A. radial drilling machine   B. shaper
    C. planer   D. lathe

22. The MAXIMUM number of 65-pound castings which can be safely raised, 22._____
    using a hoist having a 1,200-pound capacity, is
    A. 22   B. 20   C. 18   D. 16

23. The device used on a milling machine to divide the circumference of a 23._____
    piece of work into any number of equal parts is called a(n)
    A. taper attachment   B. index head
    C. face plate   D. dead center

24. Of the following, the MOST accurate measuring device is a   24._____
    A. folding rule
    B. cloth tape
    C. machinist's steel rule
    D. straight wooden rule

25. The material which is an alloy is   25._____
    A. copper   B. brass   C. nickel   D. silver

KEY (CORRECT ANSWERS)

1. D	11. A	21. D
2. A	12. A	22. C
3. D	13. D	23. B
4. D	14. A	24. C
5. B	15. C	25. B
6. C	16. D	
7. C	17. D	
8. B	18. C	
9. C	19. B	
10. B	20. A	

TEST 2

DIRECTIONS: Each question or incomplete statement is followed by several suggested answers or completions. Select the one that BEST answers the question or completes the statement. *PRINT THE LETTER OF THE CORRECT ANSWER IN THE SPACE AT THE RIGHT.*

Questions 1 through 10 refer to the tools shown below. Read the item, and for the operation given, select the proper tool to be used from those shown:

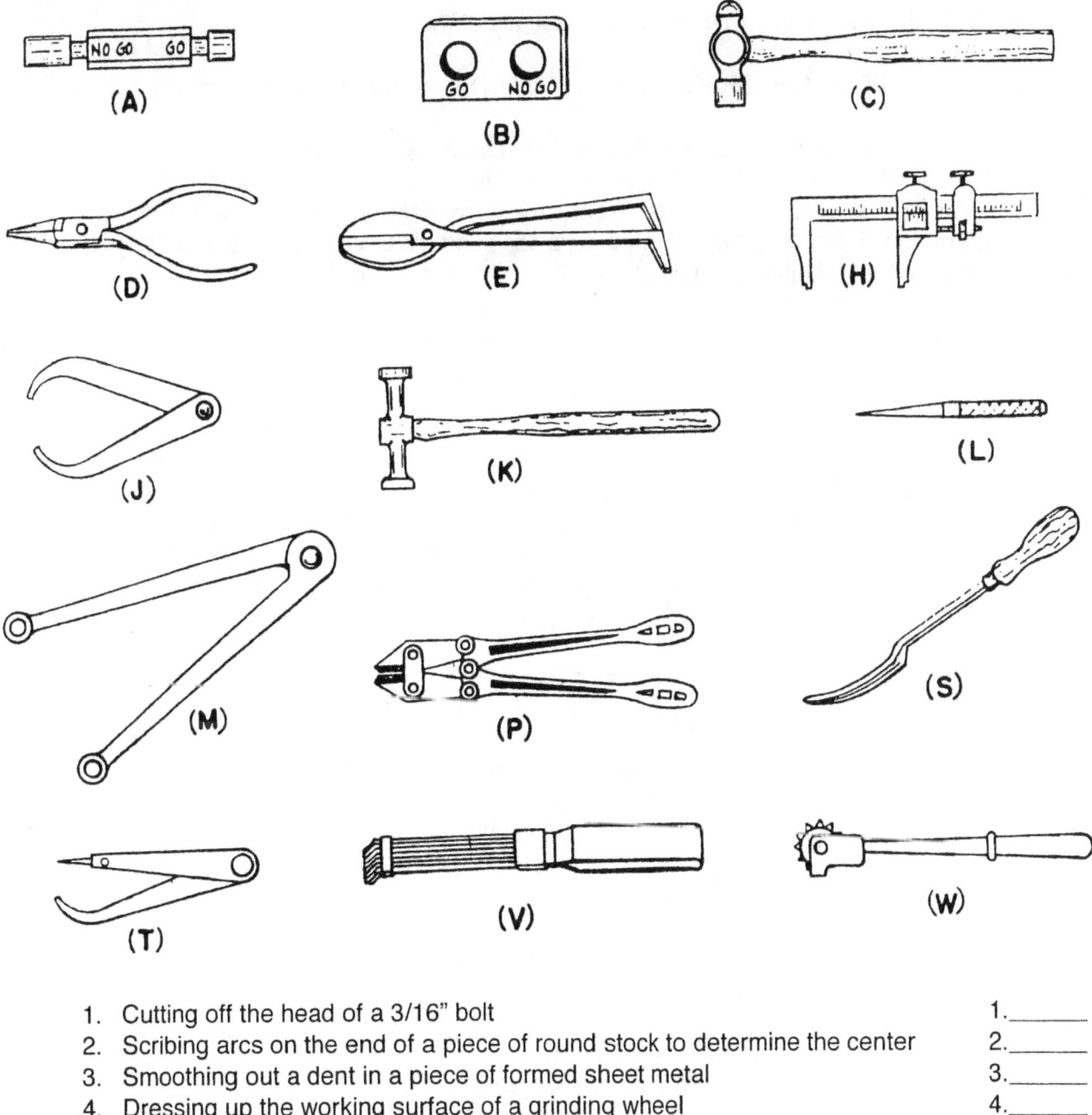

1. Cutting off the head of a 3/16" bolt 1._____
2. Scribing arcs on the end of a piece of round stock to determine the center 2._____
3. Smoothing out a dent in a piece of formed sheet metal 3._____
4. Dressing up the working surface of a grinding wheel 4._____

41

5. Quickly checking the bore of a quantity of brass bushings for proper tolerance limits 5._____
6. Peening a rivet 6._____
7. Scraping a bearing 7._____
8. Removing a large screw plug having two blind holes on the top circular surface 8._____
9. Determining the exact inside diameter of a metal tube 9._____
10. Scraping carbon off a cylinder head 10._____

Questions 11 through 18 refer to the passage below:

EDISON STORAGE BATTERY MAINTENANCE PROCEDURE

Take a voltage reading of each cell in the battery with a voltmeter. Any battery with two or more dead or reverse cells is to be removed and sent to the shop. All cell caps are to be opened and the water level brought up to 2-3/4" above the plates. Any battery requiring a considerable amount of water must be called to the foreman's attention. All cell caps must be brushed clean and special Edison battery oil applied to them. No batteries are to remain in service with cell caps broken or missing. The normal specific gravity reading of the solution must not be above 1.230 or below 1.160. This reading is to be taken only on batteries which are found to be weak. Batteries with specific gravity lower than 1.160 must be sent to the shop. Be careful when disconnecting leads from the battery, since a slight turn of the connecting post will result in a dead cell due to the cell plates becoming short-circuited. When disconnecting leads use a standard Edison terminal puller. When recording defective cells, give the battery number, car number, and the position of the cell in the battery. No. 1 cell is the cell to which the positive battery lead is connected and so on up to the last cell, No. 26, to which the negative lead is connected.

11. A normal specific gravity reading would be 11._____
    A. 1.450   B. 1.294   C. 1.200   D. 1.180

12. Batteries with below normal specific gravity reading MUST 12._____
    A. always have water added
    B. be called to the foreman's attention
    C. not be given a voltmeter test
    D. be sent to the shop

13. The battery leads are disconnected by using 13._____
    A. gas pliers
    B. Edison battery oil to free them
    C. a screwdriver to pry them off
    D. a standard Edison terminal puller

14. To completely record a defective cell
    A. only one identifying number is required
    B. two identifying numbers are required
    C. three identifying numbers are required
    D. four identifying numbers are required

15. A battery MUST be taken out of service if it has
    A. one dead cell   B. broken cell caps
    C. one reversed cell   D. a low water level

16. The battery water level should be brought up above the plates by _____ inches.
    A. 2.75   B. 1.370   C. 1.264   D. 0.600

17. Specific gravity readings are to be taken only on batteries which
    A. are removed from service
    B. have missing cell caps
    C. are weak
    D. have a high water level

18. Dead cells are sometimes caused by
    A. a slight turn of the connecting post
    B. taking unnecessary gravity readings
    C. adding too little battery oil
    D. adding too much water

19. Using only the balance weights shown below, the LEAST number of weights required for a scale to balance with a 3/4 pound load is

    | 2 OZ. |
    | 2 OZ. |
    | 3 OZ. |
    | 3 OZ. |
    | 4 OZ. |
    | 6 OZ. |

    A. 6   B. 5   C. 3   D. 1

20. One complete turn of the drum crank will move the weight vertically upward a distance of _____ feet.

20._____

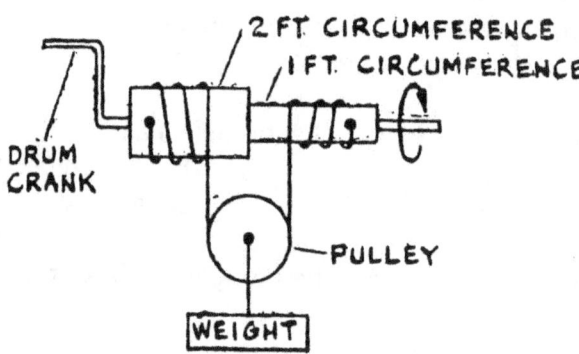

    A. 4   B. 3 1/2   C. 3   D. 1 1/2

21. The dimension "X" on the plate is

21._____

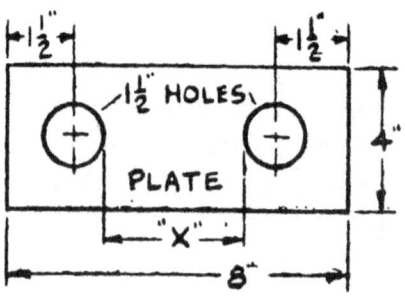

    A. 5"   B. 4"   C. 3 1/2"   D. 2 1/2"

22. In the rectangular sheet shown, the area (in square inches) of the shaded portion is

22._____

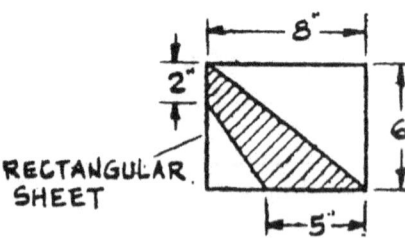

    A. 38   B. 32   C. 24   D. 18

23. If the pinion makes six complete revolutions than the gear rack will move   23._____

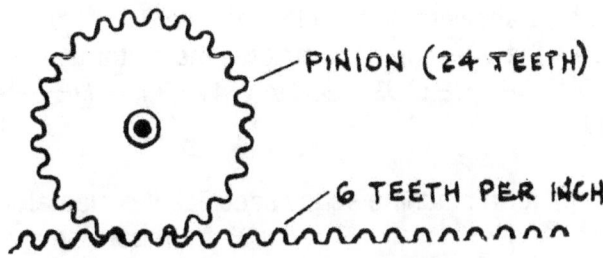

    A. 24"   B. 32"   C. 44"   D. 64"

24. The sheet metal which is MOST difficult to solder is   24._____
    A. copper   B. brass   C. aluminum   D. tin

25. Powdered graphite is a good   25._____
    A. abrasive   B. lubricant   C. adhesive   D. insulator

KEY (CORRECT ANSWERS)

1. P	11. C	21. C
2. T	12. D	22. D
3. K	13. D	23. A
4. W	14. C	24. C
5. A	15. B	25. B
6. C	16. A	
7. S	17. C	
8. M	18. A	
9. H	19. C	
10. V	20. D	

TEST 3

DIRECTIONS: Each question or incomplete statement is followed by several suggested answers or completions. Select the one that BEST answers the question or completes the statement. *PRINT THE LETTER OF THE CORRECT ANSWER IN THE SPACE AT THE RIGHT.*

1. The number 6-32 for a machine screw specifies the diameter and the
   A. length
   B. number of threads per inch
   C. type of head
   D. hardness

   1._____

2. It is undesirable to allow a soldering iron to overheat since this would cause
   A. the copper tip to harden
   B. the copper tip to soften
   C. damage to the tinned surface of the tip
   D. the soldering fumes to become poisonous

   2._____

3. A tachometer is an instrument used to measure
   A. current flow
   B. RPM
   C. water flow
   D. temperature

   3._____

4. Pipe threads are GENERALLY coated with white lead in order to
   A. compensate for expansion and contraction
   B. make the threads run easier
   C. make a tight joint
   D. quickly identify the threaded joints

   4._____

5. The PROPER tool to use when making a 1/8-inch hole in a piece of light gauge sheet metal is a(n)
   A. hand drill
   B. ratchet brace
   C. awl
   D. air drill

   5._____

6. Eyebolts are GENERALLY fastened to the shells of machines in order to
   A. act as a leveling device
   B. permit easy attachment of lifting chains
   C. permit easy tagging of equipment
   D. couple two machines together

   6._____

7. A drift pin is a tool GENERALLY used to
   A. ream holes
   B. line up holes in similar superimposed heavy plates
   C. countersink holes
   D. machine finish a drilled hole

   7._____

8. The correct speed at which to use a drill is important. In general, good practice requires the drill speed to be
    A. lower for cast iron than for brass
    B. higher for cast iron than for brass
    C. higher for mild steel than for brass
    D. the same for cast iron, brass and mild steel

8._____

9. With respect to the driving wheel, the driven wheel will rotate at

9._____

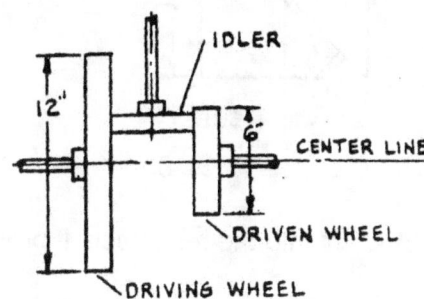

   A. twice the speed   B. 2/3 the speed
   C. 1/3 the speed   D. the same speed

10. In the combination of wheels shown, the rotating speed of wheel W is

10._____

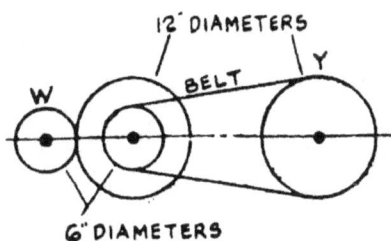

   A. 1/4 as much as wheel Y   B. 3 times that of wheel Y
   C. 4 times that of wheel Y   D. 5 times that of wheel Y

11. The number of complete turns the vise handle MUST make to fully close the jaws is

11._____

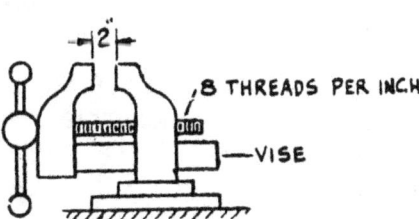

   A. 6   B. 12   C. 16   D. 24

12. The total MAXIMUM number of triangular pieces, equal in area to A or B, which can be cut from the full tin sheet is

12._____

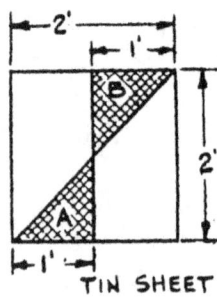

A. 3   B. 5   C. 8   D. 9

13. The male plug will PROPERLY fit into the receptacle if projection

13._____

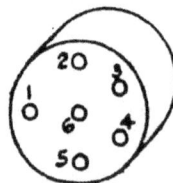 

A. 9 is lined up with hole 2
B. 11 is lined up with hole 1
C. 8 is lined up with hole 1
D. 7 is lined up with hole 2

14. A castellated nut is ESPECIALLY designed to accommodate a(n)
   A. lockwasher   B. acorn cap
   C. cotter pin   D. additional lock nut

14._____

15. Of the following, the MOST brittle material would be
   A. cast iron   B. annealed aluminum
   C. forged steel   D. rolled steel

15._____

16. When checking the diameter of a piece of round stock being turned in a lathe, it is GOOD practice to use a micrometer with the piece
   A. rotating at normal speed   B. stationary
   C. rotating at high speed   D. always out of the lathe

16._____

17. Carbon tetrachloride is useful for
   A. lubrication and rust prevention
   B. extinguishing fires and cleaning electrical parts
   C. extinguishing fires and rust prevention
   D. cleaning electrical parts and rust prevention

17._____

18. Copper tubes are often used in preference to steel pipe because the copper tubes are less likely to
    A. corrode   B. freeze   C. puncture   D. sweat

    18._____

19. Of the following, the tool which is NOT tempered is a(n)
    A. center punch
    B. hacksaw blade
    C. chisel
    D. abrasive wheel

    19._____

20. An offset box wrench is preferable to a straight box wrench for tightening a nut that
    A. has stripped threads
    B. is marred
    C. is held tight with a lockwasher
    D. has limited space in front of it

    20._____

21. The PRINCIPAL advantage of using a reversible ratchet socket wrench is that
    A. nuts cannot be overtightened
    B. it gives better leverage than any other type of wrench with the same length handle
    C. nuts can be quickly loosened and tightened in cases where a complete turn of the wrench is not possible
    D. it has fewer parts to wear compared to other wrenches

    21._____

22. A screwdriver blade in good condition should have a _____ bottom edge.
    A. rounded
    B. knife-sharp
    C. chisel-shaped
    D. flat

    22._____

23. A POOR procedure when drilling is
    A. to use cutting oil when drilling metal
    B. tilting the drill sideways to enlarge a hole
    C. tight clamping of the work
    D. setting the drill shaft tightly into the chuck

    23._____

24. Micrometers are generally kept in covered boxes MAINLY to protect them from
    A. theft
    B. humidity changes
    C. dirt and dust
    D. temperature changes

    24._____

25. In the mechanical assembly shown, an INCORRECT dimension would be   25._____

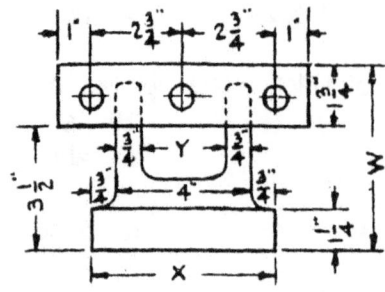

A. Y equals 2 1/2"
B. X equals 5 1/2"
C. W equals 3"
D. V equals 7 1/2"

KEY (CORRECT ANSWERS)

1. B	11. C	21. C
2. C	12. C	22. D
3. B	13. B	23. B
4. C	14. C	24. C
5. A	15. A	25. C
6. B	16. B	
7. B	17. B	
8. A	18. A	
9. D	19. D	
10. C	20. D	

TEST 4

DIRECTIONS: Each question or incomplete statement is followed by several suggested answers or completions. Select the one that BEST answers the question or completes the statement. *PRINT THE LETTER OF THE CORRECT ANSWER IN THE SPACE AT THE RIGHT.*

1. In order to properly secure the three metal pieces tightly together by means of the single machine screw a thread should be tapped in piece(s)

   1.

   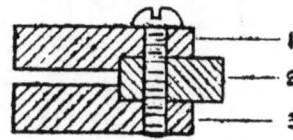

   A. 1 and 3   B. 3   C. 1   D. 2

2. If an 8" level indicates 16 quarts of oil in the tank, then the number of quarts of oil to be added to raise the level from 6" to 8" is

   2.

   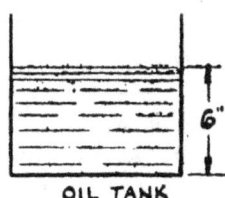

   A. 3   B. 4   C. 5   D. 7

3. In the pile of timbers shown there are fewer

   3.

   A. rectangular timbers than round timbers
   B. round timbers than rectangular timbers
   C. triangular timbers than round timbers
   D. round timbers than triangular timbers

51

4. The form shown, which is open at both ends, can be shaped from metal sheet number

4._____

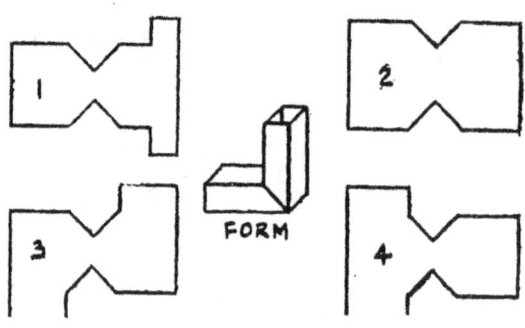

A. 2   B. 3   C. 1   D. 4

5. In order to fill the three reservoirs with air from the compressor, the LEAST number of valves to be opened or closed from their normal position is

5._____

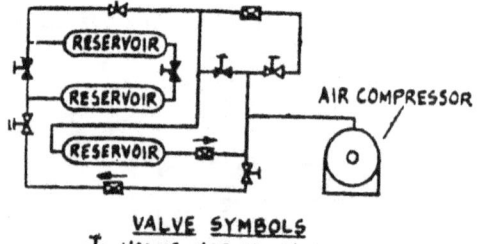

A. 1   B. 3   C. 4   D. 5

6. If the contacts come together once every second, the cam is rotating at _____ rpm.

6._____

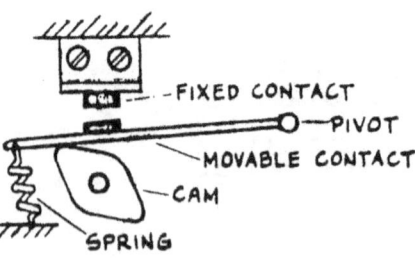

A. 30   B. 55   C. 65   D. 78

7. If the float in the tank develops a bad leak, then the   7._____

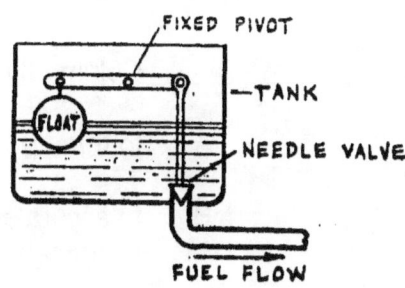

    A. flow of fuel will stop
    B. float will stay in the position shown
    C. needle valve will remain in the open position
    D. float will rise

8. A cold chisel is shown in position 1 or 2 and the grinding wheel is shown   8._____
with direction of rotations 3 or 4. To properly sharpen the cold chisel, the
CORRECT combination of position and rotation is, respectively,

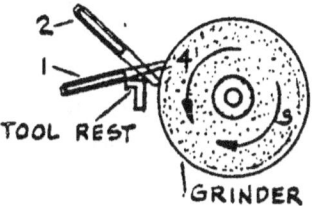

    A. 1 and 4   B. 1 and 3   C. 2 and 4   D. 2 and 3

9. The weight is to be raised by means of the rope attached to the truck. If   9._____
the truck moves forward 20 feet, then the weight will rise _____ feet.

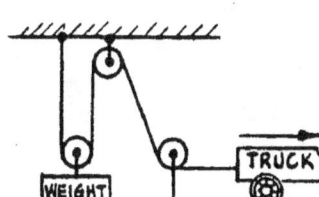

    A. 25   B. 20   C. 10   D. 4

Answer questions 10 through 19 by matching the tools in column I with the PROPER use listed in column II. Place the letter of the correct use in the space at the right.

Column I (tools and equipment)

10. Gage blocks
11. Feeler gage
12. Plumb bob
13. Dial test indicator
14. Pair of V blocks
15. Spirit level
16. Protractor
17. Carpenter's try-square
18. Concentricity gage
19. Scleroscope

Column II (use)

A. to true up work in a lathe
B. to accurately check measuring instruments
C. to hold cylindrical work in accurate alignment for drilling
D. to test hardness of metals
E. to test alignment of two holes of different diameters
H. to establish a long perpendicular line on a wall surface
J. to check a corner of a piece of work for squareness
K. to horizontally align a piece of work
L. to measure small clearances between adjacent parts
M. to establish and measure angles

10. _____
11. _____
12. _____
13. _____
14. _____
15. _____
16. _____
17. _____
18. _____
19. _____

20. Employees of the department are cautioned not to use water to extinguish fires caused by high voltage arcing. The MOST likely reason for this rule is that water
    A. may conduct the electrical current and create a shock hazard
    B. coming into contact with a hot electrical arc causes asphyxiating fumes to be generated
    C. will cause corrosion of sensitive electrical parts
    D. would cause fuses to blow in the electrical circuits

20. _____

5 (#4)

21. From the standpoint of management, the MOST desirable characteristic in a newly appointed helper would be
   A. the lack of outside personal interests
   B. the ability to keep to himself and away from the other employees
   C. the ability to satisfactorily perform his assigned duties
   D. eagerness to ask questions about all phases of the work

21._____

22. There are a few workers who are seemingly prone to accidents and who, regardless of their assigned job, have a higher accident rate than the average worker. If your coworker is known to be such an individual, the BEST course for you to pursue would be to
   A. do most of the assigned work yourself
   B. refuse to work with this individual
   C. provide him with a copy of all rules and regulations
   D. personally check all safety precautions on each job

22._____

23. The MOST logical method to use in providing shop employees with quick assistance in the case of minor injuries is to
   A. instruct most of the employees in first-aid techniques
   B. have at least two or three doctors always on the premises
   C. provide every employee with a first-aid kit
   D. have at least two or three nurses always ready to render assistance

23._____

24. Tolerances on machine work are USUALLY expressed in _____ of an inch.
   A. millionths
   B. thousandths
   C. hundredths
   D. tenths

24._____

25. Goggles are NOT necessary when
   A. welding
   B. burning with an oxy-acetylene torch
   C. soldering copper plates
   D. grinding a tool on an emery wheel

25._____

KEY (CORRECT ANSWERS)

1. B	11. L	21. C
2. B	12. H	22. D
3. C	13. A	23. A
4. B	14. C	24. B
5. A	15. K	25. C
6. A	16. M	
7. C	17. J	
8. A	18. E	
9. C	19. D	
10. B	20. A	

EXAMINATION SECTION
TEST 1

DIRECTIONS: Each question or incomplete statement is followed by several suggested answers or completions. Select the one that BEST answers the question or completes the statement. *PRINT THE LETTER OF THE CORRECT ANSWER IN THE SPACE AT THE RIGHT.*

1. The practice of placing extra weight on the rear of a fork-lift truck which is carrying an overload is

    A. *undesirable*, because the operator has too much balancing to do
    B. *undesirable,* because it puts a strain on the motor, tires, and axle of the truck
    C. *desirable,* because this prevents the truck from turning over
    D. *desirable,* because more material can be transported at a time

2. Of the following, the MOST important reason for not letting oil rags accumulate in an open storage bin is that they

    A. may start a fire by spontaneous combustion
    B. will drip oil onto other items in the bin
    C. may cause a foul odor
    D. will make the area messy

3. The decimal equivalent of 5/64 is MOST NEARLY

    A. 0.065   B. 0.068   C. 0.075   D. 0.078

4. The sum of 3 1/2", 4 1/8", and 6 3/16" is

    A. 13 3/4"   B. 13 13/16"   C. 13 7/8"   D. 13 15/16"

5. Of the following, the BEST method to employ in putting out a gasoline fire is to

    A. use a bucket of water
    B. smother it with rags
    C. use a carbon dioxide extinguisher
    D. use a carbon tetrachloride extinguisher

6. Assume that you have to move ten 65-pound crates a distance of approximately 350 feet and each crate measures 14" x 26" x 32".
   From among the following methods, it would BEST to

    A. load the crates on a pallet and use a forklift truck
    B. carry one crate at a time by yourself
    C. load the crates on a skid and use pipe rollers to move the skid
    D. unpack each crate and move all of the contents with a motor van

7. Of the following, the BEST reason for stacking long rectangular tubes in layers, with the first layer lengthwise and the next layer crosswise, is that it

    A. reduces the overall stacking height
    B. makes it simpler to count the tubes

C. makes it easier to remove a tube from the center of the stack
D. prevents the stack of tubes from toppling

8. The ACCEPTED practice for a person to follow in lifting a heavy object off the floor is to

   A. keep both legs straight and close together, and to bend at the waist to grasp the object
   B. get a solid footing, and with both legs straight, bend at the waist and lift the object
   C. place the feet as far apart as possible and bend at the knees to reach down to grasp the object
   D. place the feet shoulder-width apart and bend at the knees to reach down to grasp the object

8._____

9. When a new shipment of material is received, it is sometimes necessary to store the new material in such a way that the old stock will be used first. It is MOST important to use this method with material that

   A. is ordered in large quantities
   B. is large in size
   C. is not used often
   D. deteriorates with age

9._____

10. If a certain type of material is packaged in a container which has written on it the words *Net weight 15 pounds,* it means that the _____ 15 pounds.

    A. material alone weighs
    B. container alone weighs
    C. material and the container together weigh
    D. capacity of the container is limited to

10._____

11. Of the following, the BEST reason for storing small items, such as nails, in their original containers whenever possible is that it

    A. makes it easier to inspect these items
    B. eliminates the need for bins and shelves
    C. makes it simpler to identify these items
    D. reduces the loss of the item due to theft

11._____

12. Of the following, the one that is a grease fitting is a _____ fitting.

    A. Brown   B. Zerk   C. Taper   D. Morse

12._____

13. Of the following, the BEST tool to use to make a hole in a concrete floor for a machine hold-down is a

    A. counterboring tool   B. cold chisel
    C. drift punch   D. star drill

13._____

14. Of the following, the BEST type of saw to use to cut a 4-inch diameter hole through a 5/8-inch wooden partition is a _____ saw.

    A. back   B. saber
    C. circular   D. cross-cut

14._____

15. When removing a shrink-fitted collar from a shaft, it would be EASIEST to drive out the shaft after

    A. heating only the collar
    B. heating only the shaft
    C. chilling only the collar
    D. chilling the collar and heating the shaft

16. Of the following, the BEST reason for overhauling a machine on a regular basis is

    A. that overhauling is easier to do when done often
    B. to minimize breakdowns of the machine
    C. to make sure the machine is properly lubricated
    D. to make sure the employees are familiar with the machine

17. While using a hacksaw to cut through a one-inch diameter steel bar, a helper should not press down too heavily on the hacksaw because this may

    A. break the blade
    B. overheat the bar
    C. permanently distort the frame
    D. cause the hacksaw to flip

18. A miter box is used

    A. for locating dowel holes in two pieces of wood to be joined together
    B. to hold a saw at a fixed angle while sawing
    C. to hold a saw while sharpening its teeth
    D. to clamp two pieces of wood together at 90 degrees

19. Wing nuts are ESPECIALLY useful on equipment where

    A. the nuts must be removed frequently and easily
    B. the nuts are locked in place with a cotter pin
    C. critical adjustments are to be made frequently
    D. a standard hex head wrench cannot be used

20. The BEST device to employ to make certain that two points, separated by an unobstructed vertical distance of 12 feet, are in the BEST possible vertical alignment is a

    A. carpenter's square
    B. level
    C. folding ruler
    D. plumb bob

21. In a shop, snips should be used to

    A. hold small parts steady while machining them
    B. cut threaded pipe
    C. cut thin gauge sheet metal
    D. remove nuts that are seized on a bolt

22. Caulking a joint means

    A. applying sealing material to the joint
    B. tightening the joint with wrenches
    C. opening it with wrenches
    D. testing the joint for leaks

23. When storing files, the MOST important reason for making sure that the files do not touch each other is to prevent

    A. damage to the file teeth
    B. damage to the file stands
    C. rusting of the files
    D. dirt from accumulating in the file teeth

24. A clutch is a device that is used

    A. to hold a work piece in a fixture
    B. for retrieving small parts from hard to reach areas
    C. to disengage one rotating shaft from another
    D. to level machinery on a floor

25. Of the following, the BEST device to use to determine whether the surface of a work bench is horizontal is a

    A. surface gage   B. spirit level
    C. dial vernier   D. profilometer

KEY (CORRECT ANSWERS)

1. B	11. C
2. A	12. B
3. D	13. D
4. B	14. B
5. C	15. A
6. A	16. B
7. D	17. A
8. D	18. B
9. D	19. A
10. A	20. D

21. C
22. A
23. A
24. C
25. B

TEST 2

DIRECTIONS: Each question or incomplete statement is followed by several suggested answers or completions. Select the one that BEST answers the question or completes the statement. *PRINT THE LETTER OF THE CORRECT ANSWER IN THE SPACE AT THE RIGHT.*

1. Of the following, the machine screw having the SMALLEST diameter is the

    A. 10-24 x 3/4" B. 6-32 x 1 1/4"
    C. 12-24 x 1"   D. 8-32 x 1 1/2"

2. When drilling into a steel plate, the MOST likely cause for the breaking of a drill bit is

    A. too low a drill speed
    B. excessive cutting oil lubricant
    C. too much drill pressure
    D. using a bit with a dull point

3. Of the following, the MOST important advantage of a ratchet wrench over an open-end wrench is that the ratchet wrench

    A. can be used in a more limited space
    B. measures the torque applied
    C. will not strip the threads of a bolt
    D. is available for all sizes of hex bolts

4. The sum of 5 feet 4 1/4 inches, 8 feet 7 1/2 inches, and 13 feet 5 3/4 inches is _____ feet _____ inches.

    A. 26; 6 3/4   B. 27; 5 1/2
    C. 27; 7 1/2   D. 28; 8 3/4

5. If the floor area of one shop is 17 feet by 19 feet 3 inches and the floor area of an adjacent shop is 22 feet by 28 feet 6 inches, then the TOTAL floor area of these two shops is MOST NEARLY _____ square feet.

    A. 856   B. 946   C. 948   D. 954

6. A carton contains 9 dozen drill bits.
If a helper removes 73 drill bits, the number of bits remaining in the carton is

    A. 27   B. 35   C. 47   D. 62

7. The nominal voltage of the *D* size dry-cell battery used in common hand-held flashlights is MOST NEARLY _____ volt(s).

    A. 1   B. 1.5   C. 2.0   D. 2.5

8. In an electric circuit, a volt-ohmmeter can be used to DIRECTLY measure

    A. inductance   B. power
    C. resistance   D. capacitance

9. An ammeter is a device used for measuring the

   A. current in an electric circuit
   B. dimensions of small mechanical parts
   C. voltage in an electric circuit
   D. depth of holes

10. The purpose of a water trap in a plumbing drainage system is to

    A. prevent the leakage of water
    B. prevent freezing of the pipes
    C. block off sewer gas
    D. reduce the water pressure in the system

11. Small leaks in a compressed air pipe line leading from a shop compressor are MOST easily located by

    A. creating a vacuum in the air line
    B. allowing the compressor to pump water through the lines
    C. monitoring air gauges throughout the piping system
    D. applying soapy water to the pipeline

12. A helper is paid at the rate of $5.04 per hour and receives time and one-half for any hours he works over 40 hours.
    If he works 50 hours during a certain work week, his GROSS earnings should be

    A. $252.00   B. $262.20   C. $277.20   D. $302.40

13. Tubing with an outside diameter of 2" and a wall thickness of 1/16" has an inside diameter which is

    A. 1 1/2"   B. 1 3/4"   C. 1 7/8"   D. 1 15/16"

14. The tool that holds the die when threading pipe is GENERALLY called a

    A. vise   B. stock   C. yoke   D. coupling

15. A fitting used to join a small pipe at right angles to the middle of a large pipe is called a

    A. union
    B. coupling
    C. cap
    D. reducing tee

16. Gaskets are COMMONLY used between the flanges of large pipe joints to

    A. make a leakproof connection
    B. provide for expansion
    C. provide space for assembly
    D. adjust for poor alignment

17. The pipe fitting that should be used to connect a 1" pipe to a 1 1/2" valve is called a

    A. reducing coupling
    B. nipple
    C. bushing
    D. union

18. To prevent damage to an air compressor, the air coming into the compressor is USU-   18.____
    ALLY

    A. cooled   B. heated   C. expanded   D. filtered

19. A steel rod having a diameter of 2 1/4 inches is to be discarded when its diameter is worn   19.____
    down more than .075 inches.
    The MINIMUM diameter permissible for this rod is _____ inches.

    A. 1.175   B. 2.000   C. 2.175   D. 2.235

20. The reason for galvanizing sheet metal is to   20.____

    A. make it harder
    B. increase its tensile strength
    C. prevent it from being a conductor of electricity
    D. make it rust-resistant

21. A hole drilled in a shaft would PROBABLY be reamed to fit a   21.____

    A. lag screw   B. cap screw
    C. carriage bolt   D. taper pin

22. The part of a drill press which is used to hold the drill bit is called a   22.____

    A. chuck   B. collar   C. bit   D. vise

23. When administering first aid to a helper suffering from shock as a result of falling off a   23.____
    high ladder, it is MOST important to

    A. cover the helper and keep him warm
    B. give the helper something to drink
    C. apply artificial respiration to the helper
    D. prop the helper up to a sitting position

24. Safety shoes usually have the *unique* feature of   24.____

    A. extra hard heels and soles to prevent nails from piercing the shoes
    B. special leather to prevent the piercing of the shoes by falling objects
    C. a metal guard over the toes which is built into the shoes
    D. a non-slip tread on the heels and soles

25. If a co-worker's clothing gets caught in the gears of a machine in operation, the FIRST   25.____
    thing for a helper to do is to

    A. call the supervisor
    B. try to pull him out
    C. shut off the machine's power
    D. jam a metal tool between the gears of the machine

26. Of the following, the MOST important factor contributing to a helper's safety on the job is   26.____
    for him to

    A. work slowly   B. wear gloves
    C. be alert   D. know his job well

27. If it is necessary for you to lift one end of a piece of heavy equipment with a crow bar in order to allow a maintainer to work underneath it, the BEST of the following procedures to follow is to

    A. support the handle of the bar on a box
    B. insert temporary blocks to support the piece
    C. call the supervisor to help you
    D. wear heavy gloves

28. The part of a bus that allows one rear wheel to turn faster or slower than the other when turning a corner is the

    A. universal joint
    B. rear axle
    C. idler
    D. differential

29. In a 4-stroke cycle diesel engine, the fuel is ignited by means of

    A. compressed air at a high temperature
    B. special spark plugs
    C. cold spark plugs
    D. hot spark plugs

30. The basic purpose of an idler gear in a gear train is to

    A. change gear speed
    B. increase gear torque
    C. reduce friction in the gear train
    D. change the direction of rotation of a shaft

KEY (CORRECT ANSWERS)

1.	B	16.	A
2.	C	17.	C
3.	A	18.	D
4.	B	19.	C
5.	D	20.	D
6.	B	21.	D
7.	B	22.	A
8.	C	23.	A
9.	A	24.	C
10.	C	25.	C
11.	D	26.	C
12.	C	27.	B
13.	C	28.	D
14.	B	29.	A
15.	D	30.	D

TEST 3

DIRECTIONS: Each question or incomplete statement is followed by several suggested answers or completions. Select the one that BEST answers the question or completes the statement. *PRINT THE LETTER OF THE CORRECT ANSWER IN THE SPACE AT THE RIGHT.*

1. The jaws of a vise close 3/16 inch for each turn of the screw. 1.____
   If the vise is open 3 3/8 inches, then the number of turns needed to close the jaw is

   A. 16 B. 17 C. 18 D. 24

2. When cutting a left-hand thread on a lathe, it is NECESSARY to reverse the direction of the 2.____

   A. chuck
   B. driving motor
   C. lead screw
   D. lathe centers

3. In order to cut a 2-inch diameter hole accurately into a sheet of 16 gauge sheet metal, it is BEST to use a 3.____

   A. cutter and a bar
   B. hand reamer
   C. high speed drill
   D. nibbler

4. The instrument that is COMMONLY used to check the armature of small D.C. motors for shorts, grounds or an open circuit is a(n) 4.____

   A. ammeter
   B. dynamometer
   C. growler
   D. voltmeter

5. In some plant operations, D.C. current is required where only A.C. is supplied. A device that is used to convert the A.C. to D.C. current is called a(n) 5.____

   A. inductor coil
   B. motor-generator
   C. rheostat
   D. transformer

6. Of the following, the MOST important use for a flexible coupling is to connect two shafts which may 6.____

   A. rotate in opposite directions
   B. have different diameters
   C. occasionally become slightly misaligned
   D. rotate at different speeds

7. The PURPOSE of the packing which is generally found in the stuffing box of a centrifugal pump is to 7.____

   A. *prevent* the impeller from chattering
   B. *prevent* the leakage of fluid
   C. *reduce* bearing wear
   D. *reduce* the discharge pressure

8. A bus wheel which is unbalanced should be rebalanced by 8.____

   A. retreading the tire
   B. bending the rim slightly
   C. replacing the wheel bearing
   D. adding weights at the rim

9. *Truing* a grinding wheel refers to

   A. making the face of the wheel parallel to the spindle
   B. centering the wheel mounting hole
   C. making the face of the wheel larger
   D. mounting the wheel onto the spindle

10. If a main gear having 45 teeth is revolving at 360 RPM, then the speed of a 15-tooth pinion driving this gear is _____ RPM.

    A. 120 B. 180 C. 1080 D. 1800

11. A flux is applied during a brazing operation PRIMARILY to

    A. *prevent* fusion and penetration throughout the joint
    B. *prevent* formation of oxide films in the area of the joint
    C. *reduce* the electrical conductivity of the joint
    D. *reduce* the surface hardness in the area of the joint

12. When grinding a flat chisel, it is GOOD practice to keep the chisel moving across the face of the grinding wheel in order to prevent

    A. grooving of the wheel
    B. burning of the chisel tip
    C. the wheel from vibrating
    D. the wheel from cracking

13. If a brake drum measuring 14 9/16" I.D. is remachined to remove 60 thousandths of an inch from the diameter, the NEW diameter will measure MOST NEARLY

    A. 14.502" B. 14.563" C. 14.569" D. 14.623"

14. An electrical ballast is used in a(n)

    A. heavy duty electric power drill
    B. motor-generator set
    C. electrical circuit breaker
    D. fluorescent lighting system

15. An electrical transformer can be used to

    A. raise battery output voltage
    B. maintain constant battery output voltage
    C. lower the voltage from a 110 volt A.C. power line
    D. change the current from A.C. to D.C.

16. Metals are commonly arc-welded electrically by the use of _____ voltage and _____ current.

    A. high; high   B. high; low
    C. low; high   D. low; low

17. A pinion with 21 teeth engages a gear rack having 14 teeth per inch. When the rack has moved 1 inch, the pinion will have rotated through _____ degrees.

    A. 120 B. 180 C. 240 D. 360

Questions 18-22.

DIRECTIONS: Read the information below carefully. Then answer Questions 18 through 22 on the basis of this information.

TITANIC AIR COMPRESSOR

Valves: The compressors are equipped with Titanic plate valves which are automatic in operation. Valves are so constructed that an entire valve assembly can readily be removed from the head. The valves provide large port area with short lift and are accurately guided to insure positive seating.

Starting Unloader: Each compressor (or air end) is equipped with a centrifugal governor which is bolted directed to the compressor crank shaft. The governor actuates cylinder relief valves so as to relieve pressure from the cylinders during starting and stopping. The motor is never required to start the compressor under load.

Air Strainer: Each cylinder air inlet connection is fitted with a suitable combination air strainer and muffler.

Pistons: Pistons are lightweight castings, ribbed internally to secure strength and are accurately turned and ground. Each piston is fitted with four (4) rings, two of which are oil control rings. Piston pins are hardened and tempered steel of the full floating type. Bronze bushings are used between piston pin and piston.

Connecting Rods: Connecting rods are of solid bronze designed for maximum strength, rigidity, and wear. Crank pins are fitted with renewable steel bushings. Connecting rods are of the one-piece type, there being no bolts, nuts, or cotter pins which can come loose. With this type of construction, wear is reduced to a negligible amount, and adjustment of wrist pin and crank pin bearings is unnecessary.

Main Bearings: Main bearings are of the ball type and are securely held in position by spacers. This type of bearing entirely eliminates the necessity of frequent adjustment or attention. The crank shaft is always in perfect alignment.

Crank Shaft: The crank shaft is a one-piece heat-treated forging of best quality open-hearth steel, of rugged design, and of sufficient size to transmit the motor power and any additional stresses which may occur in service. Each crank shaft is counter-balanced (dynamically balanced) to reduce vibration to a minimum, and is accurately machined to properly receive the ball bearing races, crank pin bushing, flexible coupling, and centrifugal governor. Suitable provision is made to insure proper lubrication of all crank shaft bearings and bushings with the minimum amount of attention.

Coupling: Compressor and motor shafts are connected through a Morse Chain Company all-metal enclosed flexible coupling. This coupling consists of two sprockets, one mounted on, and keyed to, each shaft; the sprockets are wrapped by a single Morse Chain, the entire assembly being enclosed in a split aluminum grease packed cover.

18. The crank pin of the connecting rod is fitted with a renewable bushing made of

    A. solid bronze
    B. steel
    C. a slight-weight casting
    D. ball bearings

19. When the connecting rod is of the one-piece type,

    A. the wrist pins require frequent adjustment
    B. the crank pins require frequent adjustment
    C. the cotter pins frequently will come loose
    D. wear is reduced to a negligible amount

20. The centrifugal governor is bolted DIRECTLY to the

    A. compressor crank shaft
    B. main bearing
    C. piston pin
    D. muffler

21. The number of oil control rings required for each piston is

    A. one   B. two   C. three   D. four

22. The compressor and motor shafts are connected through a flexible coupling. These couplings are _____ to the shafts.

    A. keyed
    B. brazed
    C. soldered
    D. press fit

23. Before drilling a hole in a steel plate, an indentation should be made with a

    A. center punch
    B. nail
    C. drill bit
    D. pin punch

24. Of the following, the BEST way to lay out a 30-foot long straight line on a floor is to use

    A. a steel tape and carpenter's pencil
    B. chalk and a 6-foot rule
    C. chalk and a plumb bob
    D. chalk and a mason's line

25. Air supply reservoirs are generally equipped with relief valves. The PURPOSE of these valves is to

    A. compensate for air leakage from the reservoir
    B. drain water caused by condensation
    C. protect the reservoir against excessive air pressure
    D. disconnect the air supply reservoir from the supply line

KEY (CORRECT ANSWERS)

1. C
2. C
3. A
4. C
5. B

6. C
7. B
8. D
9. A
10. C

11. B
12. A
13. D
14. D
15. C

16. C
17. C
18. B
19. D
20. A

21. B
22. A
23. A
24. D
25. C

EXAMINATION SECTION
TEST 1

DIRECTIONS: Each question or incomplete statement is followed by several suggested answers or completions. Select the one that BEST answers the question or completes the statement. *PRINT THE LETTER OF THE CORRECT ANSWER IN THE SPACE AT THE RIGHT.*

Questions 1-8.

DIRECTIONS: Questions 1 through 8, inclusive, are based on the paragraph *JACKS* shown below. When answering these questions, refer to this paragraph.

JACKS

When using a jack, a workman should cheek the capacity plate or other markings on the jack to make sure the device is heavy enough to support the load. Where there is no plate, capacity should be determined and painted on the side of the jack. The workman should see that jacks are well lubricated, but only at points where lubrication is specified, and should inspect them for broken teeth or faulty holding fixtures. A jack should never be thrown or dropped upon the floors such treatment may crack or distort the metal, thus causing the jack to break when a load is lifted. It is important that the floor or ground surface upon which the jack is placed be level and clean, and the safe limit of floor loading is not exceeded. If the surface is earth, the jack base should be set on heavy wood blocking, preferably hardwood, of sufficient size that the blocking will not turn over, shift, or sink. If the surface is not perfectly level, the jack may be set on blocking, which should be leveled by wedges securely placed so that they cannot be brushed or forced out of place. "Extenders" of wood or metal, intended to provide a higher rise where a jack cannot reach up to load or lift it high enough, should never be used. Instead, a larger jack should be obtained or higher blocking which is correspondingly wider and longer — should be placed under the jack. All lifts should be vertical with the jack correctly centered for the lift. The base of the jack should be on a perfectly level surface, and the jack head, with its hardwood shim, should bear against a perfectly level meeting surface.

1. To make sure the jack is heavy enough to support a certain load, the workman should 1.____

    A. lubricate the jack
    B. shim the jack
    C. check the capacity plate
    D. use a long handle

2. A jack should be lubricated 2.____

    A. after using
    B. before painting
    C. only at specified points
    D. to prevent slipping

3. The workman should inspect a jack for 3.____

    A. manufacturer's name
    B. broken teeth
    C. paint peeling
    D. broken wedges

4. Metal parts on a jack may crack if

   A. the jack is thrown on the floor
   B. the load is leveled
   C. blocking is used
   D. the handle is too short

5. It would NOT be a safe practice for a workman to

   A. center the jack under the load
   B. set the jack on a level surface
   C. use hardwood for blocking
   D. use *extenders* to reach up to the load

6. Wedges may safely be used to

   A. replace a broken tooth
   B. prevent the overloading of a jack
   C. level the blocking under a jack
   D. straighten distorted metal

7. Blocking should be

   A. made of a soft wood
   B. placed between the jack base and the earth surface
   C. well lubricated
   D. used to repair a broken tooth

8. A hardwood shim should be used

   A. between the head and its meeting surface
   B. under the jack
   C. as a filler
   D. to level a surface

9. When a long pipe is being carried, the front end should be held high and the rear end low.
   The MAIN reason for this is to

   A. prevent injury to others when turning blind corners
   B. make it easier to carry
   C. prevent injury to the man carrying the pipe
   D. prevent damage to the pipe

10. As a serviceman, you notice a condition in the shop which you believe to be dangerous, but is under the jurisdiction of another department.
    You should

    A. immediately notify your superior
    B. call the assistant general superintendent
    C. take no action, as your department is not involved
    D. send a letter to the department involved

11. All employees should regularly read the bulletin board at their job location MAINLY in order to

    A. learn what previously posted material has been removed
    B. show that they have an interest in the department
    C. see whether other employees have something for sale
    D. become familiar with new orders or procedures posted on it

12. The book of rules and regulations states that employees must give notice, in person or by telephone, at least one hour before they are scheduled to report for duty, of their intention to be absent from work.
    The LOGICAL reason for having this rule is that

    A. the employees' time can be recorded in advance
    B. a substitute can be provided
    C. it allows time to check the employees' record
    D. it reduces absenteeism

13. When tools are found in poor condition, the reason is MOST often because of

    A. misuse of tools
    B. their use by more than one person
    C. defects in the manufacture of tools
    D. their use in construction work

14. When lifting a heavy object, a man should NOT

    A. twist his body while lifting
    B. bend knees
    C. have secure footing
    D. take a firm grip on the object

15. The MAIN purpose of the periodic inspection of machines and equipment is to

    A. locate stolen property
    B. make the workmen more familiar with the equipment
    C. discover minor faults before they develop into more serious conditions
    D. encourage the workmen to take better care of their equipment

16. If a serviceman does not understand a verbal order given him by his foreman, he should

    A. do the best he can
    B. ask for a different assignment
    C. ask the foreman to explain it
    D. look it up in the book of rules

17. A rule prohibits indulgence in intoxicating liquor, or being under its influence, while on duty. This rule is rigidly enforced in order to

    A. prevent an employee from endangering himself or others
    B. help reduce littering
    C. eliminate absenteeism
    D. help promote temperance

18. As a newly appointed serviceman, your foreman would expect you to

    A. make many blunders
    B. repair car equipment
    C. study car maintenance on your own time
    D. follow his instructions closely

19. Your work will probably be MOST appreciated by your superior if you

    A. continually ask questions about your work
    B. keep him informed whenever you think someone has violated a rule
    C. continually come to him with suggestions for improving the job
    D. do your share by completing assigned tasks properly and on time

20. One of your fellow workers has to leave work a half-hour early and asks you to punch his time card for him.
    You should

    A. punch out for him, but be sure to tell your supervisor
    B. tell him that no one is allowed to punch out someone else's time card
    C. punch out for him because you know he would do the same for you
    D. tell him he must promise to stay an extra half-hour tomorrow before you punch out for him

21. As far as is practicable, fiber rope should not be allowed to become wet, as this hastens decay. The MOST logical conclusion to be drawn from this statement is that

    A. fiber rope is stronger than nylon rope
    B. shrinkage of wet rope is not a problem
    C. nylon rope is better than wire rope
    D. wet rope should be thoroughly dried before being stored away

22. The MAIN reason that gear cases are stacked on a pallet is to

    A. help servicemen find gear cases quickly
    B. help stockmen keep track of gear cases
    C. avoid hand-carrying of gear cases
    D. prevent damage to gear cases

23. If you are holding a heavy load by the pull rope on a block and tackle, your BEST procedure is to

    A. let the rope hang loose
    B. snub the rope around a fixed object
    C. pull sideways to jam the rope in the block
    D. stand on the rope and hold the end

24. Modern electric power tools such as electric drills come with a third conductor in the power cord, which is used to connect the case of the tool to a grounded part of the electric outlet.
    The reason for this additional electrical conductor is to

A. protect the user of the tool should the motor short out to the case
B. provide for continued operation of the tool should the regular grounded line-wire open
C. eliminate sparking between the tool and the material being worked upon
D. provide a spare wire for additional controls

25. When a long ladder is being used, a length of rope should be tied from its lowest rung to a fixed support in order to prevent

    A. breaking the rungs
    B. the ladder from slipping
    C. anyone from removing the ladder
    D. anyone from walking under the ladder

26. When the level of the liquid in a storage battery on a Hi-lo truck is too low, the proper liquid to add to bring the level up to normal is

    A. salt
    B. alkaline solution
    C. acid solution
    D. distilled water

27. The MOST important reason for servicemen to keep their work areas neat and clean is that it

    A. makes more room for storage
    B. makes for happier workers
    C. prevents tools from being broken
    D. decreases the chances of accidents to workmen

28. The one of the following which is the BEST example of a material that does NOT burn easily is

    A. canvas   B. paper   C. wood   D. asbestos

29. The CHIEF reason for not letting oily rags or dust cloths accumulate in storage closets is that they

    A. look dirty
    B. may start a fire by spontaneous combustion
    C. take up space which may be used for more important purposes
    D. may drip oil onto the floor

30. The MOST logical reason for a serviceman to blow out electrical and mechanical equipment under car bodies before they are worked on by maintainers is to

    A. cool the equipment for the maintainers
    B. prevent rusting of equipment and parts
    C. prevent the maintainers from getting dirty while working
    D. prevent fires caused by heavy accumulation of dust

31. The liquid in heavy duty hydraulic jacks used in the car shops is

    A. water   B. oil   C. mercury   D. alcohol

32. It is not considered good practice to paint portable wooden ladders.
The MOST logical reason for this is that the paint

    A. would quickly wear off
    B. might hide serious defects
    C. might rub off on a supporting wall
    D. would dry out the rungs

33. In order to lift a loaded pallet overhead by means of a crane, it would be MOST desirable to use a

    A. single wire rope sling
    B. long crowbar
    C. pallet sling
    D. rope splice

34. Of the following methods, the one which is the BEST way to keep rust off metal tools is to

    A. keep them dry and oil them once in a while
    B. air blast them
    C. file or grind them often
    D. wash them carefully with warm water

35. A Hi-Lo truck delivering a compressor to a work area approaches a closed door.
The proper procedure for the Hi-Lo operator to follow is to

    A. open the door while standing on the operating end of the Hi-Lo truck
    B. open the door with the platform of the Hi-Lo truck
    C. stop the Hi-Lo truck, wedge open the door, and then proceed
    D. make a detour and follow a different path

36. The path between the two yellow lines on a main shop floor is used for

    A. picking up and discharging workers that want a ride on a Hi-Lo
    B. parking area for forklifts
    C. the traffic path for Hi-Lo's and forklifts
    D. storage of materials unloaded from Hi-Lo's

37. While on the way to a storeroom, you notice that oil has dripped on the floor from a journal box and created a slipping hazard.
You should

    A. ignore it as it is not your doing
    B. get some *speedi-dry* nearby and spread it over the oil
    C. wait until you return from the storeroom to take care of it
    D. call the supervisor and tell him about it

38. An employee always obeys the safety rules of his department because it has become a habit to work by these rules. This is

    A. *good;* such a habit will get work done safely
    B. *bad;* it is hard to change a habit
    C. *good;* safety rules won't work if they have to be thought about
    D. *bad;* safety rules should always be thought about before doing anything and not allowed to become a habit

39. If *you* are working in an inspection shop and you notice a trolley bug on one contact shoe of a car, it will mean that

    A. all contact shoes of the car are *live*
    B. only that contact shoe, that the bug is on, is *live*
    C. only the contact shoes, on the same side of the car that the bug is on, are *live*
    D. only the contact shoes of the one truck are *live*

39.____

40. It is necessary for a serviceman to wear a respirator when he is

    A. climbing a ladder
    B. operating a chipping gun
    C. blowing out the equipment under a car
    D. lubricating gear cases

40.____

KEY (CORRECT ANSWERS)

1.	C	11.	D	21.	D	31.	B
2.	C	12.	B	22.	C	32.	B
3.	B	13.	A	23.	B	33.	C
4.	A	14.	A	24.	A	34.	A
5.	D	15.	C	25.	B	35.	C
6.	C	16.	C	26.	D	36.	C
7.	B	17.	A	27.	D	37.	B
8.	A	18.	D	28.	D	38.	A
9.	A	19.	D	29.	B	39.	A
10.	A	20.	B	30.	D	40.	C

TEST 2

DIRECTIONS: Each question or incomplete statement is followed by several suggested answers or completions. Select the one that BEST answers the question or completes the statement. *PRINT THE LETTER OF THE CORRECT ANSWER IN THE SPACE AT THE RIGHT.*

1. The type of fire extinguisher which you would NOT use to extinguish a fire around electrical circuits is

    A. carbon dioxide
    B. dry chemical
    C. water
    D. dry sand

    1._____

2. Artificial respiration is applied when an accident has caused

    A. breathing difficulties
    B. loss of blood
    C. broken ribs
    D. burns

    2._____

3. Workers must NOT wear clothes that are too big when they work near moving machinery because

    A. that kind of dress will attract attention
    B. some part of the clothes can catch in the machinery
    C. big clothes get dirtier
    D. big clothes are hard to replace

    3._____

4. The MOST likely reason why an employee should make out a report after using the contents of a first aid kit is that

    A. he will learn to write a good report
    B. unauthorized use may be prevented
    C. used material will be replaced
    D. a new seal may be provided

    4._____

5. A shop employee is involved in an accident and severely injures his ankle. If a tourniquet were used, it would be to

    A. keep the ankle warm
    B. prevent infection
    C. prevent the ankle from moving
    D. stop the loss of blood

    5._____

6. If a serviceman has frequent accidents, it is MOST likely that he is

    A. a man who works best by himself
    B. satisfied with his job
    C. violating too many safety rules
    D. simply one of those persons who is unlucky

    6._____

7. In treating a cut finger, the FIRST action should be to

    A. wash it
    B. bandage it
    C. request sick leave
    D. apply antiseptic

    7._____

8. When administering first aid to a person suffering from shock as a result of an accident, it is MOST important to

    8._____

A. keep him moving
B. prop him up in a sitting position
C. apply artificial respiration
D. cover the person and keep him warm

9. First aid instructions are given to some employees to

A. eliminate the need for calling a doctor
B. prepare them to give emergency aid
C. collect blood for the blood bank
D. reduce the number of accidents

10. The BEST reason for not using compressed air from an air hose for cleaning dust from clothing is that

A. the clothing may be torn by the blast
B. it is a dangerous practice
C. this air contains too much moisture
D. the air pressure will drop too low

11. Protective helmets give servicemen the MOST protection from

A. falling objects   B. fire
C. eye injuries   D. electric shock

12. Fuses are used in electric circuits

A. so that electrical power tools cannot short circuit
B. to burn out under an overload before electrical equipment is damaged
C. to increase the amount of current that may be carried in the wires
D. so that workmen can cut off the current without looking for the switch

13. The one of the following that is MOST effective in reducing the danger from hazardous vapors is

A. immediate disposal of all wastes
B. labeling all substances clearly
C. maintaining good ventilation
D. wearing proper clothing at all times

14. A serviceman should NEVER look into the arc from an electric welding torch. The BEST reason for this is that

A. it can have a harmful effect on his eyes
B. it will distract the welder from his work
C. the serviceman is not allowed to operate a welding torch
D. electric arc welding uses a large electrical current

15. The floors of 2 cars are to be painted with a special test paint. Assume that the floor area in each car is 600 square feet. A gallon of this paint will cover 400 square feet.
The number of gallons of this paint that you should pick up at the storeroom to paint the 2 car floors would be

A. 6   B. 5   C. 4   D. 3

16. Assume that you are sent to the storeroom for 1,000 of 600-volt contact tips which are to be distributed equally to 5 foremen, but you find that the storeroom can only supply you with 825.
If you distribute these 825 tips equally to the 5 foremen, the number of tips that each foreman will receive is

   A. 165 B. 175 C. 190 D. 200

17. You are asked to fill six 5-gallon cans of oil from a full drum containing 52 gallons. When you have filled the six cans, the number of gallons of oil left in the drun will be MOST NEARLY

   A. 14 B. 16 C. 22 D. 30

18. A certain wire rope is made up of 6 strands, each strand containing 19 wires.
The total number of wires in this wire rope is

   A. 25 B. 96 C. 114 D. 144

19. The hook should be the weakest part of any crane, hoist, or sling.
According to this statement, if a particular hook has a rated capacity of 21/2 tons, then the MAXIMUM load thatshould be lifted with this hook is _____ pounds.

   A. 150 B. 3,000 C. 5,000 D. 5,500

20. Assume that 2 car wheels weigh 635 pounds each and are attached to an axle weighing 1,260 pounds.
The total weight of this assembly is MOST NEARLY _____ pounds.

   A. 1,270 B. 1,520 C. 1,895 D. 2,530

21. If an employee authorizes his employer to deduct 4% of his $450 weekly salary for a savings bond, the MINIMUM number of weekly deductions required to get enough money to buy a bond costing $54 is

   A. 3 B. 6 C. 8 D. 9

22. In weighing out a truckful of scrap metal, the scale reads 21,496 lbs. If the empty truck weighs 9,879 lbs., the amount of scrap metal, in pounds, is MOST NEARLY

   A. 10,507 B. 10,602 C. 11,617 D. 12,617

23. Four trays of material are placed on the body of a delivery truck for delivery to the inspection shop. Each tray is 4 feet wide and 4 feet long.
If these trays are placed side by side on the floor of the delivery truck, together they will cover an area of the floor MOST NEARLY _____ square feet.

   A. 32 B. 48 C. 64 D. 72

24. Assume that you are operating a degreasing tank and its tray holds 5 gear cases. It takes 40 minutes to clean one tray of gear cases.
At the end of 6 hours of operation (excluding lunch break and loading and unloading time), the number of gear cases cleaned will be

   A. 30 B. 36 C. 45 D. 50

25. If a serviceman's weekly gross salary is $480, and 20% is deducted for taxes, his take-home pay is

   A. $360 B. $384 C. $420 D. $432

26. Two-thirds of 10 feet is MOST NEARLY

   A. 6'2" B. 6'8" C. 6'11" D. 7'1"

27. You are directed to pick up a tray load of brake shoes.
    The combined weight of tray and brake shoes is 4,000 pounds. Assume that each brake shoe weighs 40 pounds and the tray weighs 240 pounds.
    The number of brake shoes in the tray is MOST NEARLY

   A. 88 B. 94 C. 100 D. 106

28. The one of the following materials that is used to protect equipment from rain is a

   A. sprinkler
   B. tarpaulin
   C. compressor
   D. templet

29. The use of wet rope near power lines and other electrical equipment is

   A. a dangerous practice
   B. sure to interrupt telephone service
   C. recommended as a safe practice
   D. common in the car shop but not in maintenance of way

Questions 30-34.

DIRECTIONS: Questions 30 through 34, inclusive, are based on the following paragraph, table, and floor plan. Each line in the table contains the name of a certain piece of car equipment together with its destination in the car shop. The floor plan shows a car shop divided into six areas, each with a different code number.

TABLE

NAME OF CAR EQUIPMENT	DESTINATION IN CAR SHOP
Journal boxes	Degreasing tanks
Door operators	Car body shop Main
Air compressors	shipping Air brake shop
Unit valves	Truck shop Degreasing
Wheels Gear assemblies	tanks Main shipping
Unit switches Variable load units	Air brake shop
Motor couplings	Degreasing tanks
Motors Brake linkage	Truck shop Degreasing
Fan motors Batteries	tanks Car body shop
Motor generators	Main shipping Car body shop

CAR SHOP FLOOR PLAN

Overhaul Shop	Air Brake Shop	Main Shipping
AREA 1	AREA 2	AREA 3
Degreasing Tanks	Truck Shop	
AREA 4	AREA 5	
Car Body Shop AREA 6		

In each of Questions 30 through 34, there are the names of four types of car equipment, and a code number for a destination in the car shop. In each question, select the CORRECT combination of equipment name and destination code number as determined by referring to the Table and Car Shop Floor Plan.

30. A. Motor generators: Area 6
    B. Fan motors: Area 5
    C. Motor couplings: Area 1
    D. Motor end housings: Area 2

31. A. Door operators: Area 3
    B. Air compressors: Area 5
    C. Brake linkage: Area 4
    D. Variable load units: Area 6

32. A. Batteries: Area 1
    B. Unit switches: Area 3
    C. Motor controllers: Area 2
    D. Fan motors: Area 4

33. A. Wheels: Area 2
    B. Motor end housings: Area 6
    C. Journal boxes: Area 3
    D. Unit valves: Area 2

34. A. Gear assemblies: Area 4
    B. Motor couplings: Area 3
    C. Variable load units: Area 6
    D. Unit valves: Area 5

35. The drawing at the right is an assembly sketch. Study the sketch and select the CORRECT assembly procedure.
    A. 3 onto 4, 2 onto 5, 1 onto 5, and tighten
    B. 4 onto 3, 1 onto 5, 5 through 4 and 3, tighten 2 onto 5
    C. 5 into 3, 2 and 1 onto 5, 4 into 3, and tighten
    D. 4 into 3, 5 through 3 and 4, 2 onto 5, 1 onto 5, and tighten

Questions 36-37.

DIRECTIONS: Questions 36 and 37 are based on the following data and sketch. When answering these questions, refer to this material.

The average clearance requirements for 2-ton, 3-ton, and 5-ton forklift trucks are shown in the following sketch. Dimensions are: R, the overall length including loads S, the overall widths T, the overall height; U, the minimum permissible width of aisle.

6 (#2)

	2-Ton Truck	3-Ton Truck	5-Ton Truck
B	112	118	142
S	45	46	47
T	85	85	85
U	76	79	92

All dimensions are in inches.

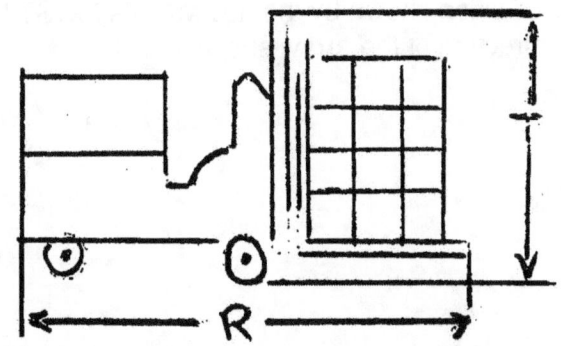

36. From the data given above, it can be seen that the overall length, including load, of a 3-ton truck is _____ inches.

    A. 85   B. 92   C. 118   D. 142

37. From the data given above, it can be seen that the overall height of a 2-ton truck is _____ inches.

    A. 47   B. 76   C. 79   D. 85

38.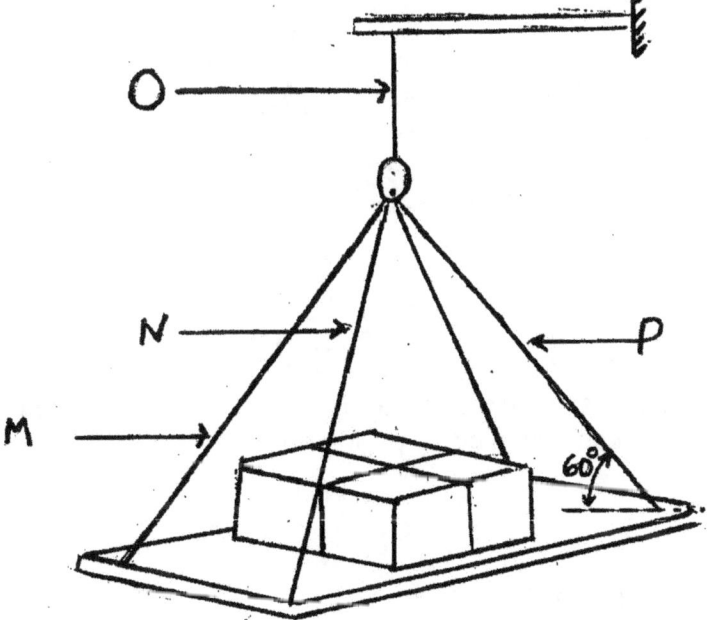

The above diagram shows a loaded sling suspended from a crane. The rope which carries the heaviest load is

    A. M   B. N   C. O   D. P

39. If the tray shown in the diagram at the right is being pushed in the direction shown by the arrows, it is MOST likely to move in the direction of the arrow shown in

39._____

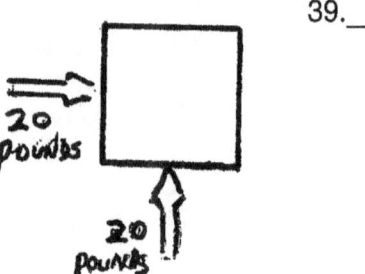

A. 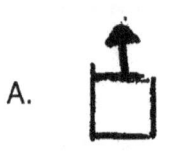   B.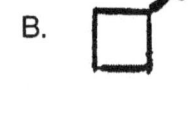

C.    D.

40._____

40.

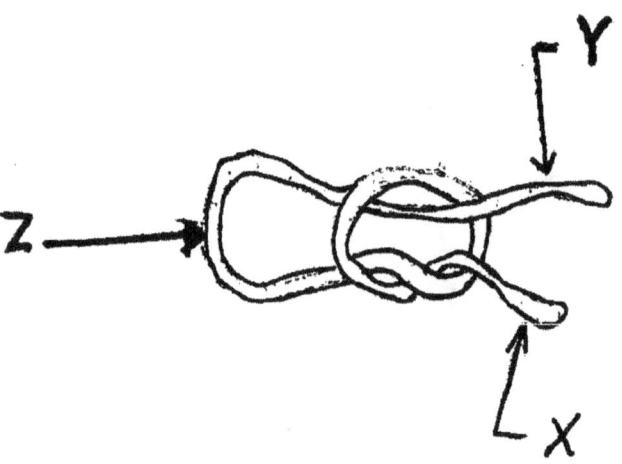

The above diagram shows a slip knot. The way this knot is nade, it would be CORRECT to say that the knot can be untied by pulling on line _____ while holding _____.

A. X; line Z
B. Y; line X
C. X and line Y together; line Z
D. Z; lines X and Y together

KEY (CORRECT ANSWERS)

1. C	11. A	21. A	31. C
2. A	12. B	22. C	32. B
3. B	13. C	23. C	33. D
4. C	14. A	24. C	34. A
5. D	15. D	25. B	35. D
6. C	16. A	26. B	36. C
7. A	17. C	27. B	37. D
8. D	18. C	28. B	38. C
9. B	19. C	29. A	39. B
10. B	20. D	30. A	40. B

EXAMINATION SECTION
TEST 1

DIRECTIONS: Each question or incomplete statement is followed by several suggested answers or completions. Select the one that BEST answers the question or completes the statement. *PRINT THE LETTER OF THE CORRECT ANSWER IN THE SPACE AT THE RIGHT.*

1. To check whether the working surface of a machine is horizontal, it is BEST to use a 1.____

    A. straight edge B. surface gage
    C. spirit level D. plumb bob

2. The BASIC function of an idler gear in a gear train is to change 2.____

    A. from rotary motion to linear motion
    B. direction of rotation
    C. speed of rotation
    D. from linear motion to rotary motion

3. A ½-inch portable electric drill machine, rated for one horsepower, will NOT 3.____

    A. be powerful enough to drill into a concrete wall
    B. be powerful enough to drill into a steel plate
    C. drill a hole larger than ½" diameter
    D. hold a drill with a shank larger than ½" diameter

4. Of the following screws, the one that has the LARGEST outside diameter is 4.____

    A. 10-32 x 3" B. 12-24 x 1¼"
    C. 12-28 x 1½" D. 1/4-20 x 2"

5. The ADVANTAGE of using a wrench with a ratchet handle for tightening a nut is that 5.____

    A. a greater amount of force can be applied
    B. there is less probability of rounding the corners of the nut
    C. there is less probability of the wrench slipping off the nut
    D. the socket does not have to be raised off the nut to get another *bite*

6. The PROPER instrument to use for measuring the thickness of a piece of shim stock is a 6.____

    A. feeler gage B. height gage
    C. standard micrometer D. protractor

7. A drill gage is used for measuring a drill 7.____

    A. angle of twist B. cutting angle
    C. speed D. diameter

8. The liquid in the heavy duty lifting jacks used in shops is 8.____

   A. alcohol   B. mercury   C. oil   D. water

9. A gear box has been reassembled and the gears do not turn freely. 9.____
   It is ADVISABLE to

   A. check each gear mesh for backlash
   B. connect the input shaft to a motor and run-in the gears
   C. completely disassemble the gearbox and replace all of the gears
   D. work the gears free with short blows from a babbit hammer

10. When lifting a heavy object, a maintainer should 10.____

    A. bend at the waist   B. keep both feet together
    C. keep his back straight   D. keep his arms extended

11. Assume that your foreman asks you to use a newly designed machine for resurfacing 11.____
    brake drums.
    Of the following, the information that your foreman would probably be MOST interested
    in obtaining from you would be the _____ the new machine.

    A. space requirements for
    B. power requirements for
    C. best maintenance procedure for
    D. increase in production obtained with

12. Hand taps for cutting threads are generally grouped in sets of three. 12.____
    In order to tap a thread to the bottom of a blind hole in a steel block, these taps are
    usually used in the following order:_____ tap.

    A. Plug tap, taper tap, bottoming
    B. Taper tap, plug tap, bottoming
    C. Taper tap, bottoming tap, plug
    D. Bottoming tap, taper tap, plug

13. A type of stone which is frequently used to sharpen tools is 13.____

    A. carborundum   B. pumice
    C. sandstone   D. soapstone

14. Gage blocks are used for checking the accuracy of 14.____

    A. manometers   B. torque wrenches
    C. micrometers   D. thermometers

15. In order to release a tapered shank drill from the drilling machine spindle, it is BEST to 15.____
    use a hammer and a drill

    A. bit   B. center punch
    C. drift   D. chuck

16. Repeated use of a machinist's hammer frequently results in uneven face wear. 16.____
    In order to recondition the face of the hammer, it would be BEST to use a(n)

    A. file   B. grinder
    C. milling machine   D. anvil

17. The BEST tool to use for cutting copper tubing with a .030 inch wall thickness is a   17.____

    A. sharp chisel
    B. hacksaw with a fine tooth blade
    C. coarse file
    D. pair of tin shears

18. The PRIMARY purpose of the spiral flutes on a twist drill is to   18.____

    A. carry the chips away from the point
    B. increase the cutting speed of the drill
    C. improve the accuracy of drilling
    D. prevent the drill from wandering off the center line

19. The reading on the 0 to 1 inch micrometer shown is MOST NEARLY   19.____

    A. 0.125
    B. 0.224
    C. 0.254
    D. 0.285

20. The BEST time to inspect grinding machine wheels for flaws is   20.____

    A. before starting the machine
    B. after the wheel has been dressed
    C. every three months
    D. at the end of each job

21. A chamfer is usually machined on the end of a piece of round bar stock before cutting threads on the bar stock. The PURPOSE of this chamfer is to   21.____

    A. carry the chips away from the die
    B. make the bar stiffer
    C. start the threads square with the center line
    D. protect the cutting edges of the cutting die

22. A multimeter or multitester is often used in troubleshooting of electrical problems. This type of instrument can measure _____ and voltage.   22.____

    A. wattage, current,
    B. inductance, capacitance,
    C. capacitance, resistance,
    D. current, resistance,

23. Assume that you are on your way to the locker room after completing your tour and you notice that oil has dripped onto the floor, creating a slipping hazard. You should   23.____

    A. call the location chief and tell him about it
    B. ignore it since it is not in your work area
    C. get some *speedi-dry* from a nearby supply and spread it over the oil
    D. wait until you return from the locker room to take care of it

24. All repair shop employees should develop good habits concerning safe work practices. In order to develop these good habits, it would be BEST for a maintainer continually to

    A. experiment with new methods and learn from his mistakes
    B. observe the other maintainers and do what everyone else does
    C. attend classroom lectures and write everything down
    D. listen to the instructions from his foreman and follow them

25. One common cause of accidents in the repair shop is that

    A. critical parts are kept locked in storage areas
    B. emergencies frequently require changes in work schedules
    C. certain tools are overhauled instead of being replaced regularly
    D. materials are left on the floor instead of in designated storage areas

---

KEY (CORRECT ANSWERS)

1. C		11. D	
2. B		12. B	
3. D		13. A	
4. D		14. C	
5. D		15. C	
6. C		16. B	
7. D		17. B	
8. C		18. A	
9. A		19. C	
10. C		20. A	

21. C
22. D
23. C
24. D
25. D

EXAMINATION SECTION
TEST 1

DIRECTIONS: Each question or incomplete statement is followed by several suggested answers or completions. Select the one that BEST answers the question or completes the statement. *PRINT THE LETTER OF THE CORRECT ANSWER IN THE SPACE AT THE RIGHT.*

1. On an engine lathe, the saddle is a part which

   A. is attached to the tailstock
   B. rotates and holds the faceplate
   C. slides along the ways
   D. houses the back gears

   1.____

2. To facilitate milling cast iron, it is BEST to use

   A. an emulsion of soluble oil and water as a lubricant
   B. an emulsion of soluble oil and water with a small percentage of soda as a lubricant
   C. lard oil as a lubricant
   D. no lubricant

   2.____

3. When using a milling machine in a machine shop, a MAJOR difference of climb milling as compared to standard milling is that climb milling

   A. uses more power
   B. produces a better finish
   C. uses a downward cut
   D. uses cutters with less rake

   3.____

4. In an automotive gasoline engine, the camshaft is used PRIMARILY to

   A. drive the transmission
   B. operate the valve lifters
   C. change the reciprocating motion of the pistons to rotary motion
   D. operate the choke mechanism

   4.____

5. A magnetic motor starter is to be controlled with momentary start-stop pushbuttons at two locations.
   The number of control wires required, respectively, in the conduit between the controller and the first station and in the conduit between the two stations is _____ and _____.

   A. 3;3   B. 4; 4   C. 3; 4   D. 2; 4

   5.____

6. The type of fitting to use to join a 1 inch branch compressed air, pipe line to a 2 inch main air line is a

   A. reducing valve   B. reducing coupling
   C. reducing tee   D. street elbow

   6.____

7. If steel weighs 0.30 pounds per cubic inch, then the weight of a 2 inch square steel bar 90 inches long is _____ pounds.

   A. 27   B. 54   C. 108   D. 360

   7.____

91

8. In arc welding, the filler metal is provided PRIMARILY by

   A. the metal to be welded
   B. a second rod of filler metal
   C. the slag
   D. the electrode

9. Oil or grease should NOT be applied to the oxygen valve of an oxyacetylene torch PRIMARILY because this can

   A. produce an explosion hazard
   B. corrode the valve
   C. give an incorrect pressure reading
   D. make the valve too slippery to handle

10. The PRIMARY function of the thermostat in the cooling system of an automobile engine is to

    A. control the operating temperature of the engine
    B. keep the operating temperature of the engine as low as possible
    C. provide the proper amount of heat for the heater
    D. retain engine heat when the engine gets hot

11. The PRIMARY purpose of the condenser in the ignition circuit of a gasoline engine is to

    A. boost the ignition voltage
    B. rectify the ignition voltage
    C. adjust the coil voltage
    D. reduce arcing at the distributor breaker points

12. The PRIMARY purpose of the differential in the rear drive train of an automotive vehicle is to allow each of the rear wheels to

    A. rotate at different speeds
    B. go in reverse
    C. rotate with maximum torque
    D. absorb road shocks

13. When grinding a fillet weld smooth, it is best NOT to grind

    A. after the weld has cooled off
    B. slowly
    C. too much of the weld material away
    D. the surface smooth

14. When using a hand file to finish a round piece of wood rod held between lathe centers, it is usually BEST to

    A. hold the file handle with one hand and to guide the file with the other hand
    B. use the file with the lathe not rotating
    C. hold the file with one hand and guide the workpiece with the other hand
    D. use a file without a handle

15. If the voltage on a 3-phase squirrel case induction motor is reduced to 90% of its rating, the starting current

    A. increases slightly
    B. is unchanged
    C. decreases 10%
    D. decreases 20%

16. If the voltage on a 3-phase squirrel case induction motor is reduced to 90% of its rating, the full load current

    A. decreases slightly
    B. is unchanged
    C. increases 10%
    D. increases 20%

17. When laying brick, the PRIMARY reason for wetting the brick before laying it is that

    A. the brick will absorb less water from the mortar and form a better bond
    B. wet bricks are easier to position
    C. wet bricks take less time to form a bond to mortar
    D. less cement is needed in the mortar

18. Concrete is a mixture that NORMALLY consists of cement,

    A. sand, and water
    B. sand, mortar, and water
    C. gravel, and water
    D. sand, gravel, and water

19. A type of rivet which can be put in place even when a worker does NOT have access to the back side of the work is known as a _____ rivet.

    A. *bucking*
    B. *double-head*
    C. *pop*
    D. *side*

20. The fraction which is equal to 0.875 is

    A. 7/16
    B. 5/8
    C. 3/4
    D. 7/8

21. When fabricating forms for pouring concrete, the MAIN advantage of using plywood sheets over sheets made of pine boards is that plywood

    A. doesn't splinter
    B. is lighter
    C. is less expensive
    D. resists warping better

22. When chipping concrete with a pneumatic hammer, the MOST important safety item that a man should wear is

    A. goggles
    B. gloves
    C. a hard hat
    D. rubber boots

23. It is considered POOR practice to paint a wooden ladder PRIMARILY because the

    A. paint will wear off in time
    B. rails will become susceptible to damage
    C. paint will shorten the life of the rungs
    D. paint can hide serious defects

24. A concrete wall is 36' long, 9' high, and 1 1/2' thick. The number of cubic yards of concrete that were needed to make this wall is

    A. 14
    B. 18
    C. 27
    D. 36

25. Before disassembling a complex mechanical machine, a mechanic may use a center punch to make adjacent punch marks on two or more of the parts in the machine in order to

    A. mark each part as he removes it
    B. check the hardness of the parts
    C. loosen the parts
    D. give himself a guide for correct reassembly

26. From among the following tools, the BEST one to use in cutting off a section of 4-inch cast iron pipe would be a

    A. hammer and chisel   B. pneumatic hammer
    C. hammer and star drill   D. hacksaw

27. The MOST important reason for removing pressure from an air hose before breaking a hose connection is to avoid

    A. damage to the air compressor
    B. losing air
    C. damage to the hose connection
    D. personal injury

28. When using a rope fall to lower a heavy load vertically, the strain on the hand line can be reduced and the load lowered more safely if the

    A. rope is wound three or four times around a fixed post
    B. rope is lightly greased
    C. rope is held very tightly in the sheaves of the fall
    D. sheaves of the fall are small in diameter

29. Oil is frequently applied to the inside of forms prior to pouring concrete in them in order to

    A. make the concrete flow better
    B. make stripping easier
    C. keep the moisture in the concrete
    D. protect the forms

30. The instrument generally used to determine the specific gravity of a lead-acid storage battery is the

    A. ammeter   B. voltmeter   C. ohmmeter   D. hydrometer

31. A tachometer is an instrument that is used to measure

    A. horizontal distances
    B. radial distances
    C. current in electric circuits
    D. motor speed

32. If the centers of a lathe are out of line when turning a cylindrical piece, it will cause

    A. the centers to be damaged
    B. a spiral groove to be cut on the piece

C. the cutting tool to be damaged
D. the piece to have a taper

33. A low reading on the oil pressure gauge of a gasoline engine may mean that the

    A. engine bearings are too tight
    B. crankcase oil level is too low
    C. transmission oil level is too low
    D. transmission oil needs changing

34. Although cloth tapes are used for taking measurements in many kinds of work, they should NOT be used when taking accurate measurements PRIMARILY because

    A. small changes in the amount of pull on these tapes can make a big difference in the reading
    B. the numbers become worn easily and are thus difficult to read
    C. small temperature changes cause large changes in readings
    D. there are too few subdivisions of each inch on these tapes

35. When painting walls with two coats of paint, a different color is used for each coat PRIMARILY to

    A. check for full coverage by the second coat
    B. provide a better appearance
    C. lower the painting cost
    D. allow the painter to use any color paint for the first coat

36. To drill a hole in the same place on a number of identical steel parts, it is BEST to use a

    A. blanking tool   B. punch press
    C. counterbore   D. jig

37. The MAIN purpose of a chuck on a lathe is to

    A. hold the workpiece
    B. hold the cutting tool
    C. allow speed changes to be made
    D. allow screw threads to be turned

38. The metal which has the GREATEST resistance to the flow of electricity is

    A. steel   B. copper   C. silver   D. gold

39. Tinning a soldering iron means

    A. applying flux to the tip
    B. cleaning the tip to make it bright
    C. applying a coat of solder to the tip
    D. heating the iron to the proper temperature

40. A protractor is an instrument that is used to   40._____
    A. measure the thickness of shims
    B. drill blind holes
    C. measure angles
    D. drill tapped holes

KEY (CORRECT ANSWERS)

1. C	11. D	21. D	31. D
2. D	12. A	22. A	32. D
3. C	13. C	23. D	33. B
4. B	14. A	24. B	34. A
5. C	15. C	25. D	35. A
6. C	16. C	26. A	36. D
7. C	17. A	27. D	37. A
8. D	18. D	28. A	38. A
9. A	19. C	29. B	39. C
10. A	20. D	30. D	40. C

TEST 2

DIRECTIONS: Each question or incomplete statement is followed by several suggested answers or completions. Select the one that BEST answers the question or completes the statement. *PRINT THE LETTER OF THE CORRECT ANSWER IN THE SPACE AT THE RIGHT.*

1. Common nail sizes are designated by

    A. penny size
    B. weight
    C. head size
    D. shank diameter

    1._____

2. Toggle bolts should be used to fasten conduit clamps to a _____ wall.

    A. concrete
    B. hollow tile
    C. brick
    D. solid masonry

    2._____

3. Backlash in a pair of meshed gears is defined as the

    A. distance between the gear centers
    B. gear ratio of the pair
    C. wear of the teeth
    D. *play* between the gear teeth

    3._____

4. Relief valves on an air supply reservoir are used for the purpose of

    A. protecting the reservoir against excessively high pressures
    B. compensating for air leakage from the reservoir
    C. retaining the air in the reservoir
    D. draining moisture from the reservoir

    4._____

5. Of the following, the BEST tool to use for securely tightening a one-inch standard hexagonal nut is a(n)

    A. monkey wrench
    B. open-end wrench
    C. Stillson wrench
    D. pair of heavy duty pliers

    5._____

6. The type of pipe which is MOST likely to be broken by careless handling is one made of

    A. copper   B. steel   C. brass   D. cast iron

    6._____

7. Open-end wrenches are usually made with the sides of the jaws at about a 15 degree angle to the centerline of the handle.
   The PURPOSE of this type of design is that it

    A. increases the leverage of the wrench
    B. enables the wrench to lock on to the bolt head
    C. is useful when using the wrench in close quarters
    D. prevents extending the handle with a piece of pipe

    7._____

8. The type of tool which is used with a portable electric drill to cut 2-inch diameter circular holes in wood is the

    A. reamer
    B. twist drill
    C. hole saw
    D. circular saw

    8._____

9. For a certain job, you will need 25 steel bars 1 inch in diameter and 4'6" long. If these bars weigh 3 pounds per foot of length, then the TOTAL weight for all 25 bars is _____ pounds.

   A. 13.5   B. 75.0   C. 112.5   D. 337.5

10. If the allowable load on a wooden scaffold is 60 pounds per square foot and the scaffold surface area is 3 feet by 12 feet, then the MAXIMUM total distributed load that is permitted on the scaffold is _____ pounds.

    A. 720   B. 1800   C. 2160   D. 2400

11. If the floor area of one shop is 15' by 21'3" and the size of an adjacent shop is 18' by 30'6", then the TOTAL floor area of these two shops is _____ square feet.

    A. 1127.75   B. 867.75   C. 549.0   D. 318.75

12. To make certain that two points separated by a vertical distance of 8 feet are in exact vertical alignment, it would be BEST to use a

    A. plumb bob
    C. protractor
    B. spirit level
    D. mason's line

13. An offset screwdriver is MOST useful for turning a wood screw when

    A. the screw is large
    B. space above the screw is limited
    C. the screw is the Phillips type
    D. the screw must be tightened very securely

14. If an 8-32 x 11" machine screw is not available, the screw which could MOST easily be modified to use in an emergency is the

    A. 8-36 x 1"
    C. 6-32 x 1 1/2"
    B. 10-32 x 1"
    D. 8-32 x 1 1/2"

15. After a file has been used on soft material, the BEST way to clean the file is to use

    A. a file card
    C. a bench brush
    B. fine emery cloth
    D. a cleaning solution

16. The type of wrench that should be used to tighten a nut or bolt to a specified number of foot-pounds is a _____ wrench.

    A. torque   B. spanner   C. box   D. lug

17. When a hacksaw blade is turned at right angles to its holding frame, it is done PRIMARILY to

    A. increase the accuracy of cutting
    B. reduce the strain on the frame
    C. cut more rapidly
    D. make cuts which are deeper than the frame

18. The PRIMARY purpose of galvanizing steel is to

    A. increase the strength of the steel
    B. provide a good base for painting

C. prevent rusting of the steel
D. improve the appearance of the steel

19. When installing a heavy new machine in a shop, the BEST way to level the machine on the shop floor is to

    A. use steel shims under the feet
    B. use a thin layer of cement under the feet
    C. grind the feet of the machine to suit
    D. install adjustable shock mounts

20. The type of valve that permits fluid to flow in one direction ONLY in a pipe run is a _____ valve.

    A. check   B. gate   C. globe   D. cross

21. If the scale on a shop drawing is 1/2 inch to the foot, then the length of a part which measures 4 1/4 inches long on the drawing has a length of APPROXIMATELY _____ feet.

    A. 2 1/8   B. 4 1/4   C. 8 1/2   D. 10 3/4

22. It is important to use safety shoes PRIMARILY to guard the feet against

    A. tripping hazards   B. heavy falling objects
    C. shock hazards   D. mud and dirt

23. When using a wrench to tighten a bolt, it is considered BAD practice to extend the handle of the wrench with a pipe for added leverage PRIMARILY because

    A. the pipe may break
    B. the bolt head may be broken off
    C. more space will be needed to turn the wrench with the pipe on it
    D. no increase in leverage is obtained in this manner

24. To accurately measure the small gap between relay contacts, it is BEST to use a(n)

    A. depth gauge   B. *GO-NO GO* gauge
    C. feeler gauge   D. inside caliper

25. The plumbing symbol shown on the right represents a
    A. steam trap
    B. coupling
    C. cross fitting
    D. valve

26. On oxyacetylene welding equipment, the feed pressure of the gases is reduced by means of

    A. tip valves   B. regulator valves
    C. relief valves   D. nozzle size

27. The purpose of the ignition coil in a gasoline engine is PRIMARILY to

    A. smooth the voltage   B. raise the voltage
    C. raise the current   D. smooth the current

28. The weight per foot of length of a 2" x 2" square steel bar as compared to a 1" x 1" square steel bar is _____ times as much.

    A. two B. four C. six D. eight

29. Electric arc welding is COMMONLY done using _____ amperage and _____ voltage.

    A. low; low
    B. low; high
    C. high; low
    D. high; high

30. Creosote is COMMONLY used

    A. to preserve wood
    B. to produce a good finish on wood
    C. as a primer coat of paint on wood
    D. to fireproof wood

31. The term *shipping* when applied to rope means

    A. coiling the rope in a tight ball
    B. lubricating the strands with tallow
    C. wetting the rope with water to make it easier to coil
    D. binding the ends with cord to prevent unraveling

32. Many portable electric power tools, such as electric drills, which operate on 110V A.C., have a third conductor in the power cord.
    The reason for this extra conductor is to

    A. prevent overheating of the power cord
    B. provide a spare conductor
    C. make the power cord stronger
    D. ground the case of the tool

33. The sum of 4 feet 3 1/4 inches, 7 feet 2 1/2 inches, and 11 feet 1/4 inch is _____ feet _____ inches.

    A. 21; 6 1/4 B. 22; 6 C. 23; 5 D. 24; 5 3/4

34. The number 0.038 is read as

    A. 38 tenths
    B. 38 hundredths
    C. 38 thousandths
    D. 38 ten-thousandths

35. Assume that an employee is paid at the rate of $5.43 per hour with time and a half for overtime past 40 hours in a week.
    If he works 43 hours in a week, his gross weekly pay is

    A. $217.20 B. $219.20 C. $229.59 D. $241.64

36. Vapor lock in a vehicle with a gasoline engine is caused by excessive heat.
    To prevent vapor lock, it may be necessary to relocate the(a)

    A. ignition system
    B. cooling system
    C. starter motor
    D. part of the fuel line

37. An ohmmeter is an instrument for measuring electrical

    A. voltage B. current C. power D. resistance

38. A thermal overload device on a motor is used to protect it against 38.____

    A. high voltage
    B. over-speeding
    C. excessively high current
    D. low temperatures

39. A union is a pipe fitting that is used to join together 39.____

    A. two pipes of different diameters
    B. two pipes of the same diameter
    C. a threaded pipe to a sweated pipe
    D. two sweated pipes of the same diameter

40. If a 30 ampere fuse is placed in a fuse box for a circuit requiring a 15 ampere fuse, 40.____

    A. serious damage to the circuit may result from an overload
    B. better protection will be provided for the circuit
    C. the larger fuse will tend to blow more often since it carries more current
    D. it will eliminate maintenance problems

KEY (CORRECT ANSWERS)

1.	A	11.	B	21.	C	31.	D
2.	B	12.	A	22.	B	32.	D
3.	D	13.	B	23.	B	33.	B
4.	A	14.	D	24.	C	34.	C
5.	B	15.	A	25.	D	35.	D
6.	D	16.	A	26.	B	36.	D
7.	C	17.	D	27.	B	37.	D
8.	C	18.	C	28.	B	38.	C
9.	D	19.	A	29.	C	39.	B
10.	C	20.	A	30.	A	40.	A

EXAMINATION SECTION

TEST 1

DIRECTIONS: Each question or incomplete statement is followed by several suggested answers or completions. Select the one that BEST answers the question or completes the statement. *PRINT THE LETTER OF THE CORRECT ANSWER IN THE SPACE AT THE RIGHT.*

Questions 1-17:
Use the following diagrams of tools to answer questions 1 through 17. (Tools are NOT drawn to scale.)

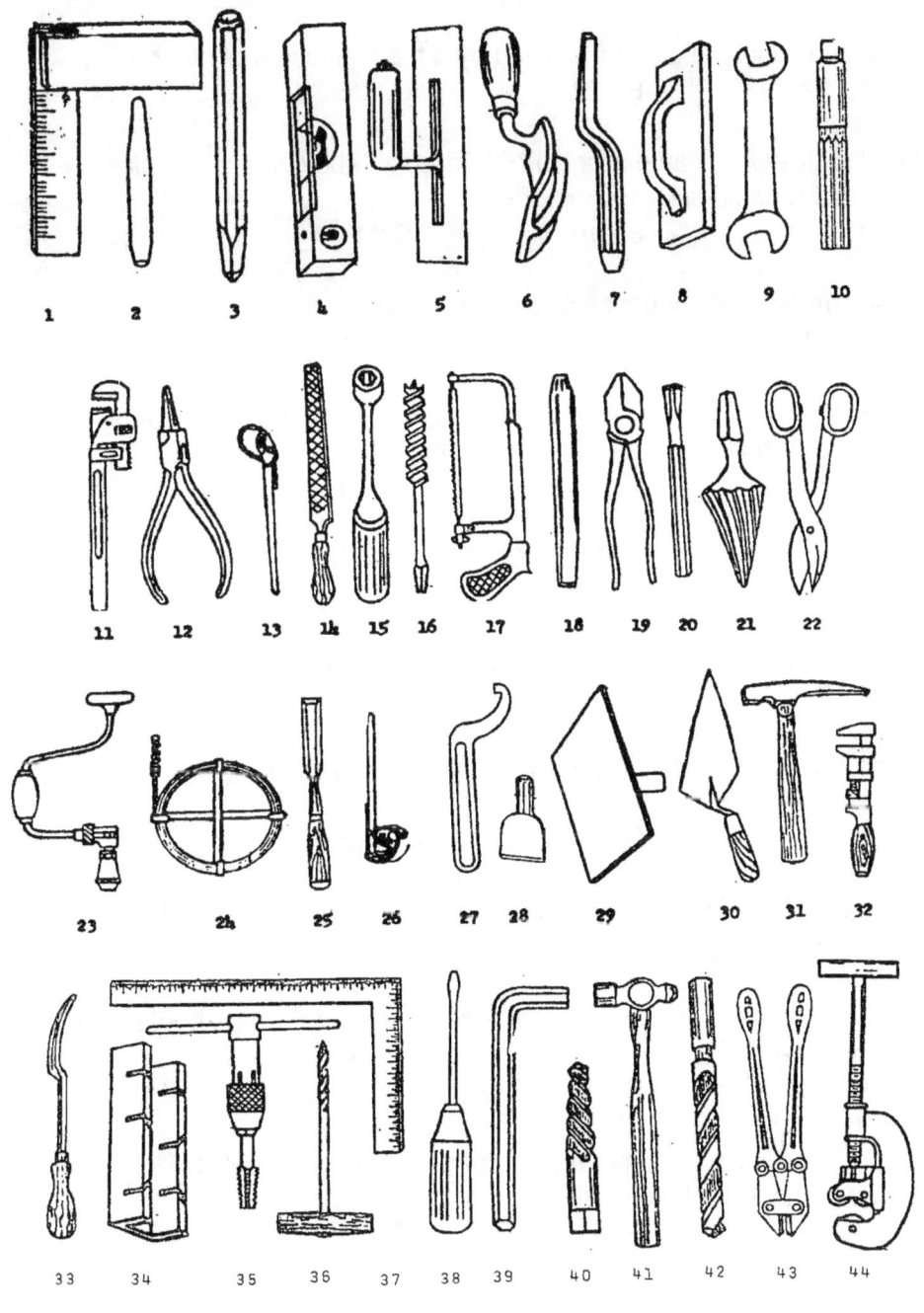

1. To tighten an elbow on a threaded pipe, a mechanic should use tool number
   A. 9   B. 11   C. 26   D. 32

   1._____

2. To cut grooves in a newly poured cement floor, a mechanic should use tool number
   A. 5   B. 6   C. 28   D. 29

   2._____

3. To "caulk" a lead joint, a mechanic should use tool number
   A. 7   B. 10   C. 25   D. 33

   3._____

4. The term "snips" should be applied by a mechanic to tool number
   A. 12   B. 22   C. 36   D. 43

   4._____

5. To slightly enlarge an existing 17/32" diameter hole in a metal plate, a mechanic should use tool number
   A. 3   B. 10   C. 14   D. 35

   5._____

6. The term "snake" should be applied by a mechanic to tool number
   A. 21   B. 23   C. 24   D. 40

   6._____

7. If the threaded portion of a 1/2" brass pipe breaks off inside a gate valve, the piece should be removed with tool number
   A. 15   B. 35   C. 39   D. 40

   7._____

8. To cut a face brick into a bat, a mechanic should use tool number
   A. 3   B. 18   C. 25   D. 28

   8._____

9. A mechanic should cut a 3" x 2" x 3/16" angle iron with tool number
   A. 3   B. 17   C. 22   D. 43

   9._____

10. A mechanic should tighten a chrome-plated water supply pipe by using tool number
    A. 11   B. 19   C. 26   D. 32

    10._____

11. The term "hawk" should be applied by a mechanic to tool number
    A. 28   B. 29   C. 30   D. 33

    11._____

12. If your coworker asks you to pass him the "star" drill, you should hand him tool number
    A. 16   B. 20   C. 40   D. 42

    12._____

13. After threading a 1" diameter piece of pipe, a mechanic should debur the inside by using tool number
    A. 14   B. 21   C. 36   D. 40

    13._____

14. A mechanic should apply the term "float" to tool number
    A. 4   B. 6   C. 8   D. 28

15. If a mechanic has to cut a dozen 15-inch lengths of 3/4" steel pipe for spacers, he should use tool number
    A. 18   B. 26   C. 43   D. 44

16. If a mechanic is erecting two structural steel plates and needs to line up the bolt holes, he should use tool number
    A. 2   B. 3   C. 33   D. 42

17. To cut reinforcing wire mesh to be used in a concrete floor, you should use tool number
    A. 7   B. 17   C. 18   D. 43

18. The MAIN reason for overhauling a power tool on a regular basis is to
    A. make the men more familiar with the tool
    B. keep the men busy during slack times
    C. insure that the tool is used occasionally
    D. minimize breakdowns

19. A mechanic should NOT press too heavily on a hacksaw while using it to cut through a steel rod because this may
    A. create flying steel particles
    B. bend the frame
    C. break the blade
    D. overheat the rod

20. Creosote is COMMONLY used with wood to
    A. speed up the seasoning   B. make the wood fireproof
    C. make painting easier   D. preserve the wood

21. A mitre box should be used to
    A. hold a saw while sharpening it
    B. store expensive tools
    C. hold a saw at a fixed angle
    D. encase steel beams for protection

22. Wood scaffold planks should be inspected
    A. at regular intervals   B. once a week
    C. before they are stored away   D. each time before use

23. Continuous sheeting should be used when excavating deep trenches in
    A. rock   B. stiff clay
    C. firm earth   D. unstable soil

24. The MAIN reason for requiring that certain special tools be returned to the tool room after a job has been completed is that
    A. missing tools can be replaced
    B. the men will not need to care for the tools
    C. more tools will be available for use
    D. this permits easier inspection and maintenance of tools

25. The BEST material to use to extinguish an oil fire is
    A. sand   B. water   C. sawdust   D. gravel

26. A "Lally" column is
    A. fabricated from angles and plates
    B. fabricated by tying two channels together with lattice bars
    C. a steel member that has unequal sections
    D. a pipe fitted with a base plate at each end

27. The BEST action for you to take if you discover a small puddle of oil on the shop floor is to first
    A. have it cleaned up
    B. find out who spilled it
    C. discover the source of the leak
    D. cover it with newspaper

28. You should listen to your foreman even when he insists on explaining the procedure for a job you have done many times before because
    A. you can do the job the way you want when he leaves
    B. he may make an error and you can show that you know your job
    C. it is wise to humor him even if he is wrong
    D. you are required to do the job the way the foreman wants it

Questions 29-34:
Answer questions 29 through 34 by referring to the sketches that follow.

29. The indicated pressure is, MOST NEARLY, _____ psi.   29._____
    A. 132   B. 137   C. 143   D. 148

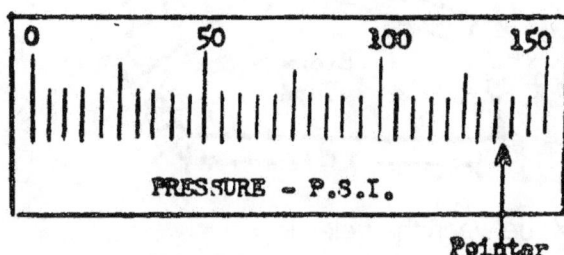

30. The LEAST number of shims, of any combination of thickness, required to   30._____
    exactly fill the 1/4" gap shown is
    A. 7   B. 8   C. 9   D. 10

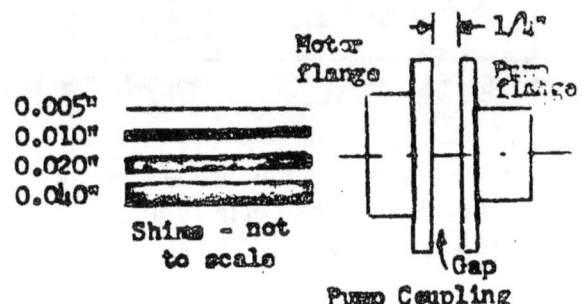

31. The dimension "X" on the keyway shown is   31._____
    A. 3-3/8"   B. 3-9/16"   C. 3-3/4"   D. 4"

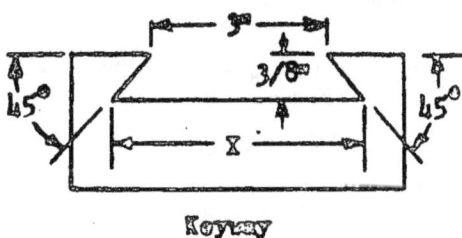

32. If the tank gauge reads 120 psi, then the pipe gauge should read ___ psi.   32._____
    A. 80   B. 120   C. 180   D. 240

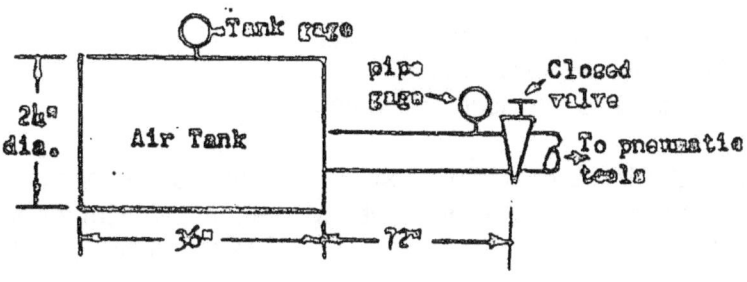

6 (#1)

33. The MINIMUM number of feet of chainlink fence needed to completely enclose the storage yard shown is
    A. 278   B. 286   C. 295   D. 304

33._____

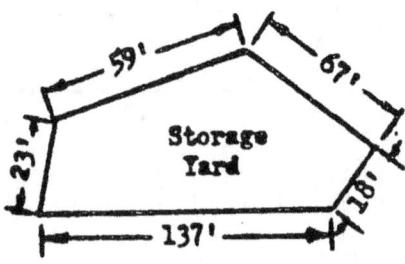

34. The distance "X" between the holes is
    A. 1-7/8"   B. 2-1/16"   C. 2-3/8"   D. 2-9/16"

34._____

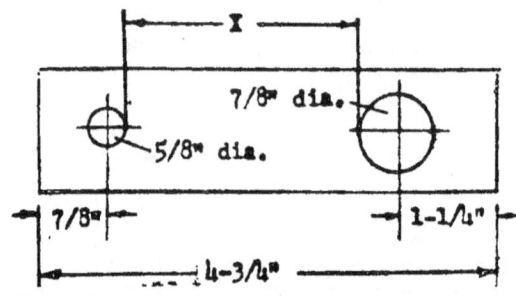

35. A rule requires all employees to report defective equipment to their superiors, even when the maintenance of the particular pieces of equipment is handled by someone else. The MAIN purpose of this rule is to
    A. determine who is doing the job improperly
    B. have repairs made before trouble occurs
    C. encourage all employees to be alert at all times
    D. reduce the cost of equipment

35._____

36. Some equipment is fitted with wing nuts. Such nuts are ESPECIALLY useful when
    A. the nut is to be wired closed
    B. space is limited
    C. the equipment is subject to vibration
    D. the nuts must be removed frequently

36._____

37. It is considered BAD practice to use water to put out electrical fires MAINLY because the water may
    A. rust the equipment
    B. short circuit the lines
    C. cause a serious shock
    D. damage the electrical insulation

37._____

38. The BEST instrument to use to make certain that two points, separated by a vertical distance of nine feet, are in perfect vertical alignment is a
    A. square   B. level   C. plumb bob   D. protractor

38._____

39. While you are being trained, you will be assigned to work with an experienced mechanic. It would be BEST for you to
    A. remind the mechanic that he is responsible for your training
    B. tell him frequently how much you know about the work
    C. let him do all the work while you observe closely
    D. be as cooperative and helpful a you can

40. If a measurement scaled from a drawing is one inch, and the scale of the drawing is 1/8 inch to the foot, then the one-inch measurement would represent an ACTUAL length of
    A. 8 feet   B. 2 feet   C. 1/8 of a foot   D. 8 inches

KEY (CORRECT ANSWERS)

1. B	11. B	21. C	31. C
2. B	12. B	22. D	32. B
3. A	13. B	23. D	33. D
4. B	14. C	24. D	34. A
5. B	15. D	25. A	35. B
6. C	16. A	26. D	36. D
7. D	17. D	27. A	37. C
8. D	18. D	28. D	38. C
9. B	19. C	29. B	39. D
10. C	20. D	30. A	40. A

TEST 2

DIRECTIONS: Each question or incomplete statement is followed by several suggested answers or completions. Select the one that BEST answers the question or completes the statement. *PRINT THE LETTER OF THE CORRECT ANSWER IN THE SPACE AT THE RIGHT.*

1. Cloth tapes should NOT be used when accurate measurements must be obtained because
    A. the numbers soon become worn and thus difficult to read
    B. there are not enough subdivisions of each inch on the tape
    C. the ink runs when wet, thus making the tape difficult to read
    D. small changes in the pull on the tape will make considerable differences in tape readings

    1._____

2. It is considered GOOD practice to release the pressure from an air hose before uncoupling the hose connection because this avoids
    A. wasting air
    B. possible personal injury
    C. damage to the air tool
    D. damage to the air compressor

    2._____

3. In brick construction, a structural steel member is used to support the wall above door and window openings. This member is called a
    A. purlin   B. sill   C. truss   D. lintel

    3._____

4. The BEST procedure to use to properly ignite an oxyacetylene cutting torch is to
    A. crack the acetylene valve, apply the spark, and open the oxygen valve
    B. crack the acetylene valve, then the oxygen valve, and apply the spark
    C. crack the oxygen valve, then the acetylene valve, and apply the spark
    D. crack the oxygen valve, apply the spark, open the acetylene valve

    4._____

5. The information in an accident report which may be MOST useful in helping to prevent similar-type accidents from happening is the
    A. cause of the accident   B. time of day it happened
    C. type of injuries suffered   D. number of people injured

    5._____

6. The MAIN reason why each coat of paint should be of a different color when two coats of paint are specified is that
    A. cheaper paint can be used as the undercoat
    B. less care need be taken in applying the coats
    C. any missed areas will be easier to spot
    D. the colors do not have to be exact

    6._____

110

7. To prevent manila hoisting ropes from raveling, the ends are
   A. moused B. whipped C. spliced D. eyed

8. The MAIN advantage of aluminum ladders over wooden ladders is that they are
   A. much stronger
   B. lighter
   C. cheaper
   D. more stable

9. The splices in columns in steel construction are USUALLY made
   A. two feet above floor level
   B. two feet below floor level
   C. at floor level
   D. midway between floors

10. Open-end wrenches with small openings are generally made shorter in overall length than open-end wrenches with larger openings. The MOST important reason for this is to
    A. save material
    B. provide compactness
    C. prevent overstressing the wrench
    D. provide correct leverage

11. Galvanized steel wire is wire that has been coated with
    A. zinc B. copper C. tin D. lead

12. "Camber" in a steel roof truss refers to the
    A. grade of steel used
    B. stress in the steel
    C. finish applied to the steel
    D. upward curve of the lower chord

13. A structural member is marked 8 WF 18. The 18 in this designation is the
    A. depth of the web
    B. width of the flange
    C. length of the member
    D. weight per foot

14. A strictly enforced safety rule in a rigging gang is that only one man gives the signals to the crane operator. However the ONE signal that anyone in the gang is allowed to give is the
    A. hoist-up signal
    B. boom-down signal
    C. swing signal
    D. stop signal

15. "Turnbuckles" are GENERALLY used to
    A. raise heavy loads
    B. splice two cables
    C. tie a cable to a column
    D. tighten a cable

16. If a mechanic opens the strands of a piece of manila rope and finds sawdust-like material inside the rope, it means the rope

    A. has dried out and must be re-oiled before use
    B. is relatively new
    C. has been damaged and should be discarded
    D. is to be used only for light loads until the sawdust has been cleaned out

16._____

Questions 17-21:
Refer to the passage below to answer questions 17 through 21.

REGULATIONS FOR SMALL GROUPS WHO MOVE FROM POINT TO POINT ON THE TRACKS

    Employees who perform duties on the tracks in small groups and who move from point to point along the trainway, must be on the alert at all times and prepared to clear the track when a train approaches without unnecessarily slowing it down. Underground at all times, and out-of-doors between sunset and sunrise, such employees must not enter upon the tracks unless each of them is equipped with an approved light. Flashlights must not be used for protection by such groups. Upon clearing the track to permit a train to pass, each member of the group must give a proceed signal, by hand or light, to the motorman of the train. Whenever such small groups are working in an area protected by caution lights or flags, but are not members of the gang for whom the flagging protection was established, they must not give proceed signals to motormen. The purpose of this rule is to avoid a motorman's confusing such signal with that of the flagman who is protecting a gang. Whenever a small group is engaged in work of an engrossing nature or at any time when the view of approaching trains is limited by reason of curves or otherwise, one man of the group, equipped with a whistle, must be assigned properly to warn and protect the man or men at work and must not perform any other duties while so assigned.

17. If a small group of men are traveling along the tracks toward their work location and a train approaches, they should

    A. stop the train
    B. signal the motorman to go slowly
    C. clear the track
    D. stop immediately

17._____

18. Small groups may enter upon the tracks

    A. only between sunset and sunrise
    B. provided each has an approved light
    C. provided their foreman has a good flashlight
    D. provided each man has an approved flashlight

18._____

4 (#2)

19. After a small group has cleared the tracks in an area unprotected by caution lights or flags, 19._____
    A. each member must give the proceed signal to the motorman
    B. the foreman signals the motorman to proceed
    C. the motorman can proceed provided he goes slowly
    D. the last member off the tracks gives the signal to the motorman

20. If a small group is working in an area protected by the signals of a track gang, the members of the small group 20._____
    A. need not be concerned with train movement
    B. must give the proceed signal together with the track gang
    C. can delegate one of their members to give the proceed signal
    D. must not give the proceed signal

21. If the view of approaching trains is blocked, the small group should 21._____
    A. move to where they can see the trains
    B. delegate one of the group to warn and protect them
    C. keep their ears alert for approaching trains
    D. refuse to work at such locations

Questions 22-28:
Refer to the sketched below to answer questions 22 through 28.

22. The distance "Y" is 22._____
    A. 5/8"   B. 7/8"   C. 1-1/8"   D. 1-3/8"

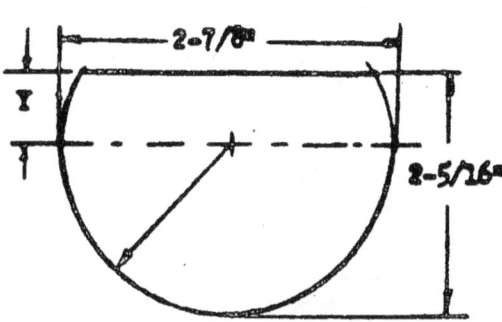

23. The sketch shows the float-operated trippers for operating a sump pump. If you want the pump to start sooner, you should 23._____
    A. lower the upper tripper   B. lower the lower tripper
    C. raise the upper tripper   D. raise the lower tripper

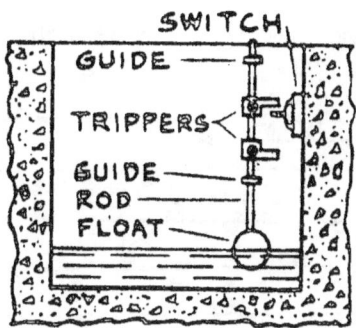

24. The width of the wood stud shown is 24._____
    A. 1-1/8"   B. 1-5/16"   C. 1-5/8"   D. 3-5/8"

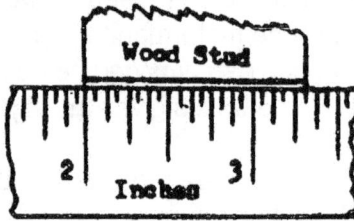

25. The right angle shown has been divided into four unequal parts. The 25._____
    number of degrees in angle "X" is
    A. 31°   B. 33°   C. 38°   D. 45°

26. The reading on the meter shown is MOST NEARLY 26._____
    A. 0465   B. 0475   C. 0566   D. 1566

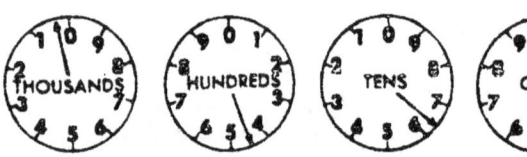

27. The length "X" of the slot shown is 27._____
    A. 2-3/8"   B. 2-7/16"   C. 2-1/2"   D. 2-9/16"

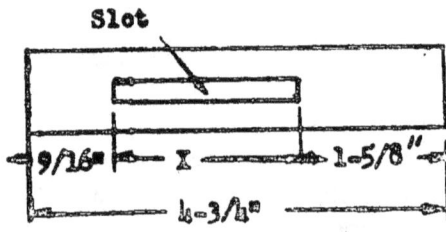

28. The volume of the bar shown is _____ cubic inches. 28._____
    A. 132   B. 356   C. 420   D. 516

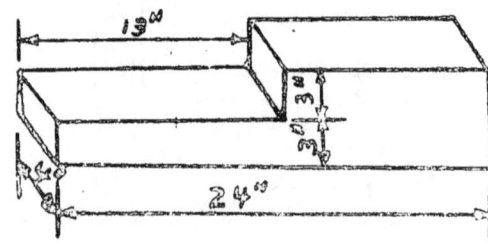

Questions 29-34:
Use the sketch below to answer questions 29 through 34.

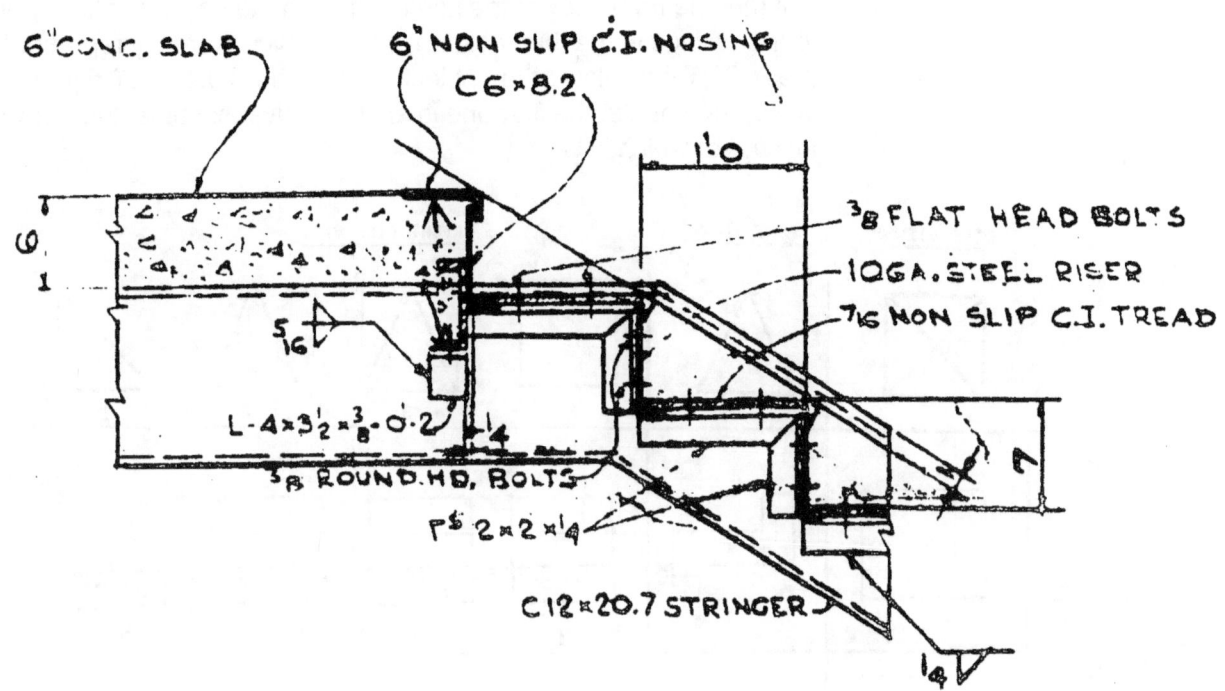

29. The stringer for this stair is a(n)
    A. I-beam   B. angle   C. H-beam   D. channel

30. The riser is made of
    A. concrete   B. sheet metal
    C. cast iron   D. wood

31. The 2 x 2 x 1/4 angles are secured to the stringer by
    A. 5/16" welds   B. 1/4" welds
    C. 3/8" flat head bolts   D. 3/8" round head bolts

32. The treads are made of
    A. concrete   B. sheet metal
    C. cast iron   D. wood

33. The height of the riser is
    A. 6"   B. 7"   C. 8"   D. 12"

34. The width of the tread is
    A. 6"   B. 7"   C. 8"   D. 12"

Questions 35-40:

DIRECTIONS: Questions 35 through 40 show the top view of an object in the first column, the front view of the same object in the second column, and four drawings in the third column, one of which correctly represents the RIGHT side view of the object. Select the CORRECT right side view. As a guide, the first one is an illustrative example, the correct answer of which is C.

35. _____

36. _____

37. _____

38. _____

39. _____

40. _____

KEY (CORRECT ANSWERS)

1. D	11. A	21. B	31. B
2. B	12. D	22. B	32. C
3. D	13. D	23. D	33. B
4. A	14. D	24. B	34. D
5. A	15. D	25. B	35. C
6. C	16. C	26. A	36. A
7. B	17. C	27. D	37. C
8. B	18. B	28. C	38. B
9. A	19. A	29. D	39. B
10. D	20. D	30. B	40. C

READING COMPREHENSION
UNDERSTANDING AND INTERPRETING WRITTEN MATERIAL
EXAMINATION SECTION
TEST 1

Questions 1-10.

DIRECTIONS: Each question or incomplete statement is followed by several suggested answers or completions. Select the one that BEST answers the question or completes the statement. *PRINT THE LETTER OF THE CORRECT ANSWER IN THE SPACE AT THE RIGHT.*

1. Accident prevention is an activity which depends for success upon factual information, research, and analysis. Experience has proved that all accidents can be prevented through the correct application of basic accident prevention methods and techniques determined from factual cause data. Therefore, to achieve the maximum results from any safety and health program, a uniform system for the reporting of accidents and causes is established. The procedures required for a report, when properly carried out, will determine accurate cause factors and the most practical methods for applying preventive or remedial action. According to the above paragraphs, which of the following statements is MOST NEARLY correct?

    A. No matter how much effort is put forth, there are some accidents that cannot be prevented.
    B. Accident prevention is a research activity.
    C. Accident reporting systems are not related to accident prevention.
    D. The success of an accident prevention program depends on the correct use of a uniform accident reporting system.

1._____

Questions 2-7.

DIRECTIONS: Questions 2 through 7 are to be answered ONLY according to the information given in the following accident report.

DATE: February 2

TO: Edward Moss, Superintendent
Pacific Houses
2487 Shell Road
Auburnsville, Illinois

SUBJECT: Report of Accident to
Philip Fay, Employee
1825 North 8th St.
Auburnsville, Ill.
Identification #374-24

Philip Fay, an employee, came to my office at 10:15 A.M. yesterday and told me that he hurt his left elbow. When I asked him what happened, he told me that 15 minutes ago, while shoveling the snow from in front of Building #14 at 2280 Stone Ave., he slipped on some snow-covered ice and fell on his elbow. Joseph Sanchez and Arthur Campbell, who were working with him, saw what happened.

119

Mr. Fay complained of pain and could not bend his left arm. I called for an ambulance right away. A police patrol car from the 85th Precinct arrived 15 minutes later, and Patrolman Johnson, Shield #8743, said that an ambulance was on the way. At 10:45 A.M., an ambulance arrived from Auburn Hospital. Dr. Breen examined Mr. Fay and told me that he would have to go to the hospital for some x-ray pictures to determine how bad the injury was. The ambulance left with Mr. Fay at 11:00 A.M.

At 3:45 P.M., Mr. Fay called from the hospital and told me that his arm had been put in a cast in the emergency room of the hospital. He was told that he had fractured his left elbow and would have to stay out of work for about four weeks. He is to report back at the hospital in three weeks for another examination and to see if the cast can be taken off. His wife was at the hospital with him, and they were now going home.

Attached are the statements from the witnesses and our completed REPORT OF INJURY form.

                                                William Fields
                                                Foreman

2. Which one of the following did NOT see the accident?

    A. Campbell   B. Fay   C. Fields   D. Sanchez

3. The CORRECT date and time of accident is February

    A. 2, 10:00 A.M.   B. 2, 10:15 A.M.
    C. 1, 10:00 A.M.   D. 1, 10:15 A.M.

4. The ambulance came about _____ hour after _____.

    A. 1/4 ; the accident   B. 1/4 ; it was called
    C. 1/2; the accident   D. 1/2; it was called

5. It is not possible to tell whether Fay went to report the accident right away because the report does NOT say

    A. how long it takes to get from Building #14 to the foreman's office
    B. how long it takes to get from Stone Ave. to Shell Rd.
    C. whether Fay telephoned the foreman first
    D. whether the foreman was in his office as soon as Fay got there

6. From the facts in the report, Fay's action might be criticized because he

    A. did not give the foreman the complete story of what had happened
    B. did not take Campbell or Sanchez with him when he went to the foreman's office in case he should need help on the way
    C. did not remain at the accident site and send Sanchez and Campbell to bring the foreman
    D. telephoned from the hospital and by using his arm to do this he might have aggravated his condition

7. Assuming that the report gives the complete story of this incident, the action of the foreman may be criticized because he did NOT

   A. call an ambulance soon enough
   B. go to the hospital with the ambulance and stay with the injured man until he was discharged
   C. have the injured man sign a release of claim against the department
   D. make an on-the-spot investigation of the accident scene nor take corrective action

Questions 8-10.

DIRECTIONS: Questions 8 through 10 are to be answered ONLY according to the information given in the following passage.

A foreman has four maintainers and two helpers assigned to him. Listed below are the maintainers and helpers and their rate of speed in completing the assignments given to them. Assume all the foreman's men (maintainers and helpers) are of equal technical ability but some work faster than others while some are slower in completing their assignments. In all cases, no overtime is to be granted.

   Maintainer E - works at average rate of speed
   Maintainer F - works at twice the rate of speed as Maintainer E
   Maintainer G - works at the same rate of speed as Maintainer E
   Maintainer H - works at half the rate of speed as Maintainer E
   Helper J - works at same rate of speed as Maintainer G
   Helper K - works at same rate of speed as Maintainer H

8. A certain job must be done immediately, and Maintainer H and Helper J are the only men available.
   If Maintainer F, working alone, could normally complete this job in six days, the TOTAL time this foreman should allot to Maintainer H and Helper J to complete the same job is _____ days.

   A. 3   B. 4   C. 8   D. 12

9. While Maintainer E and Helper J are working on a job, Helper J reports that he will be out sick for at least a week. The job normally would have taken four more days to complete, and it must be completed within these four days.
   If Maintainer H and Helper K are the only two men available, this foreman should

   A. assign Helper K to replace Helper J
   B. assign Maintainer H to replace Helper J
   C. assign both Maintainer H and Helper K to replace Helper J
   D. inform his assistant supervisor that the job cannot be completed on time

10. This foreman has assigned all six of his men to a routine maintenance job. At the end of two days, the job is four-fifths completed; and instead of reassigning all his men the following day when they would finish early, the foreman cuts the gang so that the job will take one more full day to finish. The work gang on the last day should consist of Maintainer(s)

    A. F and H
    B. F and Helper J
    C. E and Helpers J and K
    D. G and H and Helper K

Questions 11-25.

DIRECTIONS: Each question consists of a statement. You are to indicate whether the statement is TRUE (T) or FALSE (F). *PRINT THE LETTER OF THE CORRECT ANSWER IN THE SPACE AT THE RIGHT.*

Questions 11-15.

DIRECTIONS: Questions 11 through 15 are to be answered ONLY according to the information given in the following paragraph.

USING LADDERS

All ladders must be checked each day for any defects before they are used. They should not be used if there are split rails or loose rungs or if they have become shaky. Two men should handle a stepladder which is over eight feet in height, one man if the ladder is smaller. One man must face the ladder and hold it with a firm grasp while the other is working on it. When you climb a ladder, always face it, grasp the siderails, and climb up one rung at a time. You should come down the same way.

11. A ladder which is new does not have to be inspected before it is used. 11.____

12. A ladder with a loose rung may be used if this rung is not stepped on. 12.____

13. A stepladder 6 feet long may be handled by one man. 13.____

14. If a 10-foot stepladder is used, one man must hold the ladder while the other works on it. 14.____

15. The siderails of a ladder do not have to be held when climbing down. 15.____

Questions 16-20.

DIRECTIONS: Questions 16 through 20 are to be answered ONLY according to the information given in the following paragraph.

TRAFFIC ACCIDENTS

Three auto accidents happened at the corner of Fifth Street and Seventh Avenue. The first, at 7:00 P.M. last night, knocked down a light pole when two cars collided. At 8:15 A.M. this morning, two other autos crashed head on. This afternoon, at 12:30 P.M., another pair of cars crashed. One of them jumped the curb, knocked over two traffic signs, and damaged three parked cars at the corner service station. No serious injury to the drivers was reported, but all the cars involved were severely damaged.

16. Nine cars were damaged in the three accidents. 16.____

17. The three accidents happened within a period of 14 hours. 17.____

18. A service station is located at the corner of Fifth Street and Seventh Avenue. 18.____

19. In the last accident, both cars jumped the curb and knocked over two light poles. 19.____

20. The drivers of the cars in the last accident were badly hurt. 20.____

Questions 21-25.

DIRECTIONS: Questions 21 through 25 are to be answered ONLY according to the information given in the following paragraph.

LIFTING

Improper lifting of heavy objects is a frequent cause of strains and ruptures. When a heavy object is to be lifted, an employee should stand close to the object and face it squarely. The feet are spread slightly apart, and one foot is a little ahead of the other. Then, bend the knees to bring the body down to the object and keep your back comfortably vertical. Raise the object slightly to see if you can lift it alone. If you can, get a firm grasp with both hands, balance the object, and raise it by straightening the legs, but still keeping the back erect. The raising motion is gradual, not swift. In this way you use the leg muscles which are the strongest muscles in the body. This method of lifting prevents strain to the back muscles which are weak and not built for lifting purposes.

21. Many ruptures are the result of not lifting heavy objects in the correct manner. 21._____

22. When an employee lifts a heavy package, he should keep his feet close together in order to balance the load. 22._____

23. When lifting a heavy object, the back should not be bent but kept upright. 23._____

24. It is best to lift heavy objects quickly in order to prevent strains and ruptures. 24._____

25. For purposes of lifting, the leg muscles are stronger than the arm muscles. 25._____

KEY (CORRECT ANSWERS)

1.	D	11.	F
2.	C	12.	F
3.	C	13.	T
4.	D	14.	T
5.	A	15.	F
6.	B	16.	T
7.	D	17.	F
8.	C	18.	T
9.	C	19.	F
10.	B	20.	F

21. T
22. F
23. T
24. F
25. T

TEST 2

DIRECTIONS: Each question or incomplete statement is followed by several suggested answers or completions. Select the one that BEST answers the question or completes the statement. *PRINT THE LETTER OF THE CORRECT ANSWER IN THE SPACE AT THE RIGHT.*

Questions 1-8.

DIRECTIONS: Questions 1 through 8, inclusive, are based on the ladder safety rules given below. Read these rules fully before answering these questions.

LADDER SAFETY RULES

When a ladder is placed on a slightly uneven supporting surface, use a flat piece of board or small wedge to even up the ladder feet. To secure the proper angle for resting a ladder, it should be placed so that the distance from the base of the ladder to the supporting wall is one-quarter the length of the ladder. To avoid overloading a ladder, only one person should work on a ladder at a time. Do not place a ladder in front of a door. When the top rung of a ladder rests against a pole, the ladder should be lashed securely. Clear loose stones or debris from the ground around the base of a ladder before climbing. While on a ladder, do not attempt to lean so that any part of the body, except arms or hands, extends more than 12 inches beyond the side rail. Always face the ladder when ascending or descending. When carrying ladders through buildings, watch for ceiling globes and lighting fixtures. Avoid the use of rolling ladders as scaffold supports.

1. A small wedge is used to

    A. even up the feet of a ladder resting on an uneven surface
    B. lock the wheels of a roller ladder
    C. secure the proper resting angle for a ladder
    D. secure a ladder against a pole

2. An 8-foot ladder resting against a wall should be so inclined that the distance between the base of the ladder and the wall is _____ feet.

    A. 2   B. 5   C. 7   D. 9

3. A ladder should be lashed securely when

    A. it is placed in front of a door
    B. loose stones are on the ground near the base of the ladder
    C. the top rung rests against a pole
    D. two people are working from the same ladder

4. Rolling ladders

    A. should be used for scaffold supports
    B. should not be used for scaffold supports
    C. are useful on uneven ground
    D. should be used against a pole

5. When carrying a ladder through a building, it is necessary to

   A. have two men to carry it
   B. carry the ladder vertically
   C. watch for ceiling globes
   D. face the ladder while carrying it

6. It is POOR practice to

   A. lash a ladder securely at any time
   B. clear debris from the base of a ladder before climbing
   C. even up the feet of a ladder resting on slightly uneven ground
   D. place a ladder in front of a door

7. A person on a ladder should NOT extend his head beyond the side rail by more than _____ inches.

   A. 12   B. 9   C. 7   D. 5

8. The MOST important reason for permitting only one person to work on a ladder at a time is that

   A. both could not face the ladder at one time
   B. the ladder will be overloaded
   C. time would be lost going up and down the ladder
   D. they would obstruct each other

Questions 9-13.

DIRECTIONS: Questions 9 through 13 concern an excerpt of written material which you are to read and study carefully. The excerpt is immediately followed by five statements which refer to it alone. You are required to judge whether each statement

   A. is entirely true
   B. is entirely false
   C. is partly true and partly false
   D. may or may not be true but cannot be answered on the basis of the facts as given in the excerpt

It is true that in 1987 there were more strikes than in any year, excepting 1986, since 1970. However, the number of workers involved was less in 1987 than in any year since 1981, and man-days of idleness due to strikes, the MOST accurate measure of industrial strife, were less in 1987 than in any year since 1980, again excepting 1986.

9. There were fewer workers involved in strikes in 1986 than in 1981.

10. There were more strikes in 1986 than in 1987.

11. There were more strikes in 1986 than in 1970.

12. There were fewer workers involved in strikes but more man-days of idleness in 1981 than 1987.

13. There were fewer man-days of idleness and fewer workers involved in strikes in 1986 than 1987.

Questions 14-16.

DIRECTIONS: Questions 14 through 16 are to be answered on the basis of the information given in the following passage.

Telephone service in a government agency should be adequate and complete with respect to information given or action taken. It must be remembered that telephone contacts should receive special consideration since the caller cannot see the operator. People like to feel that they are receiving personal attention and that their requests or criticisms are receiving individual rather than routine consideration. All this contributes to what has come to be known as Tone of Service. The aim is to use standards which are clearly very good or superior. The factors to be considered in determining what makes good Tone of Service are speech, courtesy, understanding, and explanations. A caller's impression of Tone of Service will affect the general attitude toward the agency and city services in general.

14. The above passage states that people who telephone a government agency like to feel that they are

    A. creating a positive image of themselves
    B. being given routine consideration
    C. receiving individual attention
    D. setting standards for telephone service

15. Which of the following is NOT mentioned in the above passage as a factor in determining good Tone of Service?

    A. Courtesy   B. Education
    C. Speech   D. Understanding

16. The above passage IMPLIES that failure to properly handle telephone calls is *most likely* to result in

    A. a poor impression of city agencies by the public
    B. a deterioration of courtesy toward operators
    C. an effort by operators to improve the Tone of Service
    D. special consideration by the public of operator difficulties

Questions 17-20.

DIRECTIONS: Questions 17 through 20 are to be answered ONLY according to the information given in the following passage.

ACCIDENT PREVENTION

Many accidents and injuries can be prevented if employees learn to be more careful. The wearing of shoes with thin or badly worn soles or open toes can easily lead to foot injuries from tacks, nails, and chair and desk legs. Loose or torn clothing should not be worn near moving machinery. This is especially true of neckties which can very easily become caught in the machine. You should not place objects so that they block or partly block hallways, corridors, or other passageways. Even when they are stored in the proper place, tools, supplies, and equipment should be carefully placed or piled so as not to fall, nor have anything stick out from a pile. Before cabinets, lockers or ladders are moved, the tops should be cleared of anything which might injure someone or fall off. If necessary, use a dolly to move these or other bulky objects.

Despite all efforts to avoid accidents and injuries, however, some will happen. If an employee is injured, no matter how small the injury, he should report it to his supervisor and have the injury treated. A small cut that is not attended to can easily become infected and can cause more trouble than some injuries which at first seem more serious. It never pays to take chances.

17. According to the above passage, the one statement that is NOT true is that   17.____

   A. by being more careful, employees can reduce the number of accidents that happen
   B. women should wear shoes with open toes for comfort when working
   C. supplies should be piled so that nothing is sticking out from the pile
   D. if an employee sprains his wrist at work, he should tell his supervisor about it

18. According to the above passage, you should NOT wear loose clothing when you are   18.____

   A. in a corridor
   B. storing tools
   C. opening cabinets
   D. near moving machinery

19. According to the above passage, before moving a ladder you should   19.____

   A. test all the rungs
   B. get a dolly to carry the ladder at all times
   C. remove everything from the top of the ladder which might fall off
   D. remove your necktie

20. According to the above passage, an employee who gets a slight cut should   20.____

   A. have it treated to help prevent infection
   B. know that a slight cut becomes more easily infected than a big cut
   C. pay no attention to it as it can't become serious
   D. realize that it is more serious than any other type of injury

Questions 21-24.

DIRECTIONS: Questions 21 through 24 are to be answered on the basis of the following report.

TO: Thomas Smith   Date: June 14,
      Supervising Menagerie Keeper
                                             Subject:
FROM: Jay Jones
      Senior Menagerie Keeper

On June 14, a visitor to the monkey house at the zoo was noticed annoying the animals. He was frightening the animals by making loud noises and throwing stones at the animals in the cages. The visitor was asked to stop annoying the animals but did not. And he was then asked to leave the monkey house by the keeper on duty. The visitor would not leave and said that the zoo is public property and that as a citizen he has every right to be there. The keeper kept trying to pursuade the visitor to leave but was unsuccessful. The keeper finally threatened to call the police. The visitor soon left the monkey house and did not return. Fortunately, no animals were harmed in this incident.

21. The subject of the report has been left out.
Which one of these would be the BEST statement for the subject of the report?

    A. Loud noises in the monkey house
    B. Police called to monkey house
    C. Visitor annoying monkeys on June 14
    D. Monkeys unharmed by visitor

21._____

22. Which one of these is an important piece of information that should have been included in the FIRST sentence of the report?

    A. The kinds of monkeys in the monkey house
    B. Whether the visitor was a man or a woman
    C. The address of the monkey house
    D. The name of the zoo where the incident took place

22._____

23. The fourth sentence which begins with the words *And he was then asked...* is poorly written because

    A. the sentence begins with *And*
    B. the words *monkey house* should be written *Monkey House*
    C. the words *on duty* should be written *on-duty*
    D. *didn't* would be better than *did not*

23._____

24. In the sixth sentence, which begins with the words *The keeper kept trying...*, a word that is spelled wrong is

    A. trying   B. pursuade
    C. visitor   D. unsuccessful

24._____

Questions 25-27.

DIRECTIONS: Questions 25 through 27 test how well you can read and understand what you read. Read about ELEPHANTS. Then, on the basis of what you read, answer these questions.

ELEPHANTS

Elephants are peaceful animals and have very few real natural enemies. As with many other animals, when faced with danger the elephant tries to make himself look larger to his enemy. He does this by raising his head and trunk to look taller. The elephant will also extend his ears to look wider. Other threatening gestures may be made. The elephant may shift his weight from side to side, make a shrill scream, or pretend to charge with his trunk held high. If the enemy still fails to retreat, the elephant will make a serious attack.

25. When an elephant is in danger, he tries to make it appear that he is

    A. stronger   B. smaller   C. larger   D. angry

25._____

26. When he is threatened, an elephant tries to make himself look broader by 26._____

    A. taking a deep breath
    B. spreading out his ears
    C. shifting his weight from side to side
    D. holding his trunk high

27. If his enemy does not run away, the elephant will 27._____

    A. attack him
    B. run in the opposite direction
    C. hit the enemy with his trunk
    D. make a shrill scream

Questions 28-30.

DIRECTIONS: Read about PREVENTING DISEASE. Then, on the basis of what you read, answer Questions 28 through 30.

PREVENTING DISEASE

Proper feeding, housing, and handling are important in maintaining an animal's defenses against disease and parasites. The best diets are those that contain proteins, vitamins, minerals, and the other essential food elements. Proteins are especially important because they are necessary for growth. Minerals such as iron, copper, and cobalt help correct anemia. It has been shown that an animal's resistance can be decreased by improper feeding. However, it has not been proved that the use of certain types of feeds will increase the resistance of animals to infectious diseases. If animals are kept in good condition by proper diet and sanitary conditions, natural resistance to disease and parasites will be highest.

28. Food elements that are required especially for growth are 28._____

    A. minerals   B. vitamins
    C. proteins   D. carbohydrates

29. If animals are NOT fed correctly, they will 29._____

    A. have more diseases
    B. fight with each other
    C. need more proteins
    D. be able to kill parasites

30. The bodies of animals will BEST be able to fight disease naturally when they 30._____

    A. are kept warm
    B. are given immunity shots
    C. are given extra food
    D. have good diet and clean quarters

KEY (CORRECT ANSWERS)

1.	A	16.	A
2.	A	17.	B
3.	C	18.	D
4.	B	19.	C
5.	C	20.	A
6.	D	21.	C
7.	A	22.	D
8.	B	23.	A
9.	B	24.	B
10.	A	25.	C
11.	D	26.	B
12.	A	27.	A
13.	C	28.	C
14.	C	29.	A
15.	B	30.	D

ARITHMETICAL REASONING
EXAMINATION SECTION
TEST 1

DIRECTIONS: Each question or incomplete statement is followed by several suggested answers or completions. Select the one that BEST answers the question or completes the statement. *PRINT THE LETTER OF THE CORRECT ANSWER IN THE SPACE AT THE RIGHT.*

1. A supplier quotes a list price of $172.00 less 15 and 10 percent for twelve tools. The actual cost for these twelve tools is MOST NEARLY

    A. $146 B. $132 C. $129 D. $112

2. If the diameter of a circular piece of sheet metal is 1 1/2 feet, the area, in square inches, is MOST NEARLY

    A. 1.77 B. 2.36 C. 254 D. 324

3. The sum of 5'6", 7'3", 9'3 1/2", and 3'7 1/4" is

    A. 19'8 1/2" B. 22' 1/2" C. 25'7 3/4" D. 28'8 3/4"

4. If the floor area of one shop is 15' by 21'3" and the size of an adjacent shop is 18' by 30'6", then the TOTAL floor area of these two shops is _____ square feet.

    A. 1127.75 B. 867.75 C. 549.0 D. 318.75

5. The fraction which is equal to 0.875 is

    A. 7/16 B. 5/8 C. 3/4 D. 7/8

6. The sum of 1/2, 2 1/32, 4 3/16, and 1 7/8 is MOST NEARLY

    A. 9.593 B. 9.625 C. 9.687 D. 10.593

7. If the base of a right triangle is 9" and the altitude is 12", the length of the third side will be

    A. 13" B. 14" C. 15" D. 16"

8. If a steel bar 1" in diameter and 12' long weighs 32 lbs., then the weight of a piece of this bar 5'9" long is MOST NEARLY _____ lbs.

    A. 15.33 B. 15.26 C. 16.33 D. 15.06

9. The diameter of a circle whose circumference is 12" is MOST NEARLY

    A. 3.82" B. 3.72" C. 3.62" D. 3.52"

10. A dimension of 39/64 inches converted to decimals is MOST NEARLY

    A. .600" B. .609" C. .607" D. .611"

11. A farm worker was paid a weekly wage of $415.20 for a 44-hour work week. As a result of a new labor contract, he is paid $431.40 a week for a 40-hour work week with time and one-half pay for time worked in excess of 40 hours in any work week.
    If he continues to work 44 hours weekly under the new contract, the amount by which his average hourly rate for a 44-hour work week under the new contract exceeds the hourly rate previously paid him lies between _____ and _____, inclusive.

    A. 80¢; $1.00 B. $1.00; $1.20
    C. $1.25; $1.45 D. $1.50; $1.70

12. The sum of 4 feet 3 1/4 inches, 7 feet 2 1/2 inches, and 11 feet 1/4 inch is _____ feet _____ inches.

    A. 21; 6 1/4   B. 22; 6   C. 23; 5   D. 24; 5 3/4

13. The number 0.038 is read as

    A. 38 tenths   B. 38 hundredths
    C. 38 thousandths   D. 38 ten-thousandths

14. Assume that an employee is paid at the rate of $10.86 per hour with time and a half for overtime past 40 hours in a week.
    If he works 43 hours in a week, his gross weekly pay is

    A. $434.40   B. $438.40   C. $459.18   D. $483.27

15. The sum of the following dimensions: 3'2 1/4", 8 7/8", 2'6 3/8", 2'9 3/4", and 1'0" is

    A. 16'7 1/4"   B. 10'7 1/4"   C. 10'3 1/4"   D. 9'3 1/4"

16. Two gears are meshed together and have a gear ratio of 6 to 1.
    If the small gear rotates 120 revolutions per minute, the large gear rotates at

    A. 20   B. 40   C. 60   D. 720

17. The vacuum side of a compound gage reads 14 inches of vacuum. The barometer reading is 29.76 inches of mercury. The equivalent absolute pressure of the compound gage reading, in inches of mercury, is MOST likely

    A. 15.06   B. 15.76   C. 43.06   D. 43.76

18. The fraction 5/8 expressed as a decimal is

    A. 0.125   B. 0.412   C. 0.625   D. 0.875

19. If 300 feet of a certain size pipe weighs 450 pounds, the number of pounds that 100 feet will weigh is

    A. 1,350   B. 150   C. 300   D. 250

20. As an oiler, you work for a facility that has automobiles that use, on the average, 600 quarts of one grade of lubricating oil every month.
    The number of one-gallon cans of the above oil that should be ordered each month to meet this requirement is

    A. 100   B. 125   C. 140   D. 150

21. The inside dimensions of a rectangular oil gravity tank are: height 15", width 9", length 10".
    The amount of oil in the tank, in gallons, (231 cu.in. = 1 gallon), when the oil level is 9" high, is MOST NEARLY

    A. 2.3   B. 3.5   C. 5.2   D. 5.8

22. If 30 gallons of oil cost $76.80, 45 gallons of oil at the same rate will cost

    A. $91.20   B. $115.20   C. $123.20   D. $131.20

23. If an oiler earns $18,000 in the first six months of a year and receives a 10% raise in salary for the next six months of the same year, his TOTAL earnings for the year will be

    A. $36,000   B. $37,500   C. $37,800   D. $39,600

24. If the cost of lubricating oil increases 15%, then a gallon of oil which used to cost $10.00 will now cost MOST NEARLY

    A. $10.50   B. $11.00   C. $11.50   D. $12.00

25. The sum of 7/8", 3/4", 1/2", and 3/8" is

    A. 2 1/8"   B. 2 1/4"   C. 2 3/8"   D. 2 1/2"

KEY (CORRECT ANSWERS)

1. B
2. C
3. C
4. B
5. D

6. A
7. C
8. A
9. A
10. B

11. A
12. B
13. C
14. D
15. C

16. A
17. B
18. C
19. B
20. D

21. B
22. B
23. C
24. C
25. D

SOLUTIONS TO PROBLEMS

1. Actual cost = ($172)(.85)(.90) = $131.58 ≈ $132

2. Radius = .75', then area = (3.14)(.75)^2 ≈ 1.77 sq.ft.
   Since 1 sq.ft. = 144 sq.in., the area ≈ 254 sq.in.

3. 5'6" + 7'3" + 9'3 1/2" + 3'7 1/4" = 24'19 3/4" = 25'7 3/4"

4. Total area = (15)(21.25) + (18)(30.5) = 867.75 sq.ft.

5. .875 = 875/1000 = 7/8

6. 1 1/2 + 2 1/32 + 4 3/16 + 1 7/8 = 8 51/32 = 9 19/32 = 9.593

7. Third side = $\sqrt{9^2+12^2} = \sqrt{225}$ = 15"

8. Let x = weight. Then, 12/32 = 5.75/x. Solving, x ≈ 15.33 lbs.

9. 12" = (3.14)(diameter), so diameter ≈ 3.82"

10. $\frac{39}{64}$" = .609375" ≈ .609"

11. Under his new contract, the weekly wage for 44 hours can be found by first determining his hourly rate for the first 40 hours = $431.40 ÷ 40 ≈ $10.80. Now, his time and one-half pay will = ($10.80)(1.5) = $16.20. His weekly wage for the new contract = $431.40 + (4)($16.20) = $496.20. His new hourly rate for 44 hours = $496.20 ÷ 44 ≈ $10.34. Under the old contract, his hourly rate for 44 hours was $415.20 ÷ 44 = $9.44. His hourly rate increase = $10.34 - $9.44 = $0.90. (Answer key: between $0.80 and $1.00)

12. 4'3 1/4" + 7'2 1/2" + 11' 1/4" = 22'6"

13. .038 = 38 thousandths

14. ($10.86)(40) + ($16.29)(3) = $483.27

15. 3'2 1/4" + 8 7/8" + 2'6 3/8" + 2'9 3/4" + 1'0" = 8'25 18/8" = 10'3 1/4"

16. The gear ratio is inversely proportional to the gear size. Let x = large gear's rpm. Then, 6/1 = 120/x. Solving, x = 20

17. Subtract 14 from 29.76

18. 5/8 = .625

19. Let x = number of pounds. Then, 300/450 = 100/x. Solving, x = 150

20. 600 quarts = 150 gallons, since 4 quarts = 1 gallon

21. (9")(9")(10") = 810 cu.in. Then, 810 ÷ 231 ≈ 3.5

22. Let x = unknown cost. Then, 30/$76.80 = 45/x. Solving, x = $115.20

23. $18,000 + ($18,000)(1.10) = $37,800

24. ($10.00)(1.15) = $11.50

25. 7/8" + 3/4" + 1/2" + 3/8" = 20/8" = 2 1/2"

TEST 2

DIRECTIONS: Each question or incomplete statement is followed by several suggested answers or completions. Select the one that BEST answers the question or completes the statement. *PRINT THE LETTER OF THE CORRECT ANSWER IN THE SPACE AT THE RIGHT.*

1. A sheet metal plate has been cut in the form of a right triangle with sides of 5, 12, and 13 inches.
   The area of this plate, in square inches, is

   A. 30   B. 32 1/2   C. 60   D. 78

2. If steel weighs 480 lbs. per cubic foot, the weight of an 18" x 18" x 2" steel base plate is _____ lbs.

   A. 180   B. 216   C. 427   D. 648

3. By trial, it is found that by using 2 cubic feet of sand, a 5 cubic foot batch of concrete is produced.
   Using the same proportions, the amount of sand, in cubic feet, required to produce 2 cubic yards of concrete is MOST NEARLY

   A. 7   B. 22   C. 27   D. 45

4. The total number of cubic yards of earth to be removed to make a trench 3'9" wide, 25'0" long, and 4'3" deep is MOST NEARLY

   A. 53.1   B. 35.4   C. 26.6   D. 14.8

5. A large number of 2 x 4 studs, some 10'5" long and some 6'5 1/2" long, are required for a job.
   To minimize waste, it would be PREFERABLE to order lengths of _____ feet.

   A. 16   B. 17   C. 18   D. 19

6. A 6" pipe is connected to a 4" pipe through a reducer. If 100 cubic feet of water is flowing through the 6" pipe per minute, the flow, in cubic feet, per minute through the 4" pipe is

   A. 225   B. 100   C. 66.6   D. 44.4

7. If steel weighs 0.28 pounds per cubic inch, then the weight, in pounds, of a 2" square steel bar 120" long is MOST NEARLY

   A. 115   B. 125   C. 135   D. 155

8. A three-inch diameter steel bar two feet long weighs MOST NEARLY (assume steel weighs 480 lbs./cu.ft.) _____ lbs.

   A. 48   B. 58   C. 68   D. 78

9. The area of a circular plate will be reduced by 5% if a sector removed from it has an angle of _____ degrees.

   A. 18   B. 24   C. 32   D. 60

10. If a 4 1/16 inch shaft wears six thousandths of an inch, the NEW diameter will be _____ inches.   10.____
    A. 4.0031   B. 4.0565   C. 4.0578   D. 4.0605

11. A set of mechanical plan drawings is drawn to a scale of 1/8" = 1 foot.   11.____
    If a length of pipe measures 15 7/16" on the drawing, the ACTUAL length of the pipe is _____ feet.
    A. 121.5   B. 122.5   C. 123.5   D. 124.5

12. An electrical drawing is drawn to a scale of 1/4" = 1'. If a length of conduit on the drawing measures 7 3/8", the actual length of the conduit, in feet, is   12.____
    A. 7.5   B. 15.5   C. 22.5   D. 29.5

13. Assume that you have assigned 6 mechanics to do a job that must be finished in 4 days. At the end of 3 days, your men have completed only two-thirds of the job. In order to complete the job on time and because the job is such that it cannot be speeded up, you should assign a MINIMUM of _____ extra men.   13.____
    A. 3   B. 4   C. 5   D. 6

14. Assume that a trench is 42" wide, 5' deep, and 100' long. If the unit price of excavating the trench is $105 per cubic yard, the cost of excavating the trench is MOST NEARLY   14.____
    A. $6,805   B. $15,330   C. $21,000   D. $63,000

15. If the scale on a shop drawing is 1/4 inch to the foot, then the length of a part which measures 2 3/8 inches long on the drawing is ACTUALLY _____ feet.   15.____
    A. 9 1/2   B. 8 1/2   C. 7 1/4   D. 4 1/4

16. It is necessary to pour a new concrete floor for a shop. If the dimensions of the concrete slab for the floor are to be 27' x 18' x 6", then the number of cubic yards of concrete that must be poured is   16.____
    A. 9   B. 16   C. 54   D. 243

17. The jaws of a vise move 1/4" for each complete turn of the handle.   17.____
    The number of complete turns necessary to open the jaws 2 3/4" is
    A. 9   B. 10   C. 11   D. 12

18. Assume that a jobbing shop is to submit a price for a contract involving 300 pieces of work. Assume that material costs 50 cents per piece, labor costs $7.50 an hour, and a lathe operator can complete 5 pieces in an hour.   18.____
    If overhead is 40% of material and labor costs and the profit is 10% of all costs, the submitted price for the entire job will be
    A. $630.24   B. $872.80   C. $900.00   D. $924.00

19. The following formula is used in connection with the three-wire method of measuring pitch diameters of screw threads: $G = \dfrac{0.57735}{N}$, where G = wire size and N = number of threads per inch.
According to this formula, the proper size of wire for a 1"-8NC thread is MOST NEARLY

   A. .0722"   B. .7217"   C. .0072"   D. .0074"

20. A millimeter is 1/25.4 of an inch and there are 10 millimeters to a centimeter.
If a piece of stock measures 127 centimeters long, the length of the stock, in feet and inches, would be MOST NEARLY

   A. 2'1"   B. 4'2"   C. 8'4"   D. 41'8"

21. For a certain job, you will need 25 steel bars 1 inch in diameter and 4"6" long.
If these bars weigh 3 pounds per foot of length, then the TOTAL weight for all 25 bars is _____ pounds.

   A. 13.5   B. 75.0   C. 112.5   D. 337.5

22. If steel weighs 0.30 pounds per cubic inch, then the weight of a 2 inch square steel bar 90 inches long is _____ pounds.

   A. 27   B. 54   C. 108   D. 360

23. A concrete wall is 36' long, 9' high, and 1 1/2' thick. The number of cubic yards of concrete that were needed to make this wall is

   A. 14   B. 18   C. 27   D. 36

24. If the scale on a shop drawing is 1/2 inch to the foot, then the length of a part which measures 4 1/4 inches long on the drawing has a length of APPROXIMATELY _____ feet.

   A. 2 1/8   B. 4 1/4   C. 8 1/2   D. 10 3/4

25. If the allowable load on a wooden scaffold is 60 pounds per square foot and the scaffold surface area is 3 feet by 12 feet, then the MAXIMUM total distributed load that is permitted on the scaffold is _____ pounds.

   A. 720   B. 1,800   C. 2,160   D. 2,400

KEY (CORRECT ANSWERS)

1. A
2. A
3. B
4. D
5. B

6. B
7. C
8. A
9. A
10. B

11. C
12. D
13. A
14. A
15. A

16. A
17. C
18. D
19. A
20. B

21. D
22. C
23. B
24. C
25. C

SOLUTIONS TO PROBLEMS

1. Area = (1/2)(base)(height) = (1/2)(5")(12") = 30 sq.in.

2. Volume = (18") (18") (2") = 648 cu.in. = 648/1720 cu.ft.
   Then, (480)(648/1720) = ≈ 180 lbs.

3. 2 cu.yds. = 54 cu.ft. Let x = required cubic feet of sand. Then, 2/5 = x/54. Solving, x = 21.6 (or about 22)

4. (3.75')(25')(4.25') = 398.4375 cu.ft. ≈ 14.8 cu.yds.

5. 10'5" + 6'5 1/2" = 16'10 1/2", so lengths of 17 feet are needed

6. The amount of water flowing through each pipe must be equal.

7. (2")(2")(120") = 480 cu. in. Then, (480)(.28) ≈ 135 lbs.

8. Volume = (π) (.125 ')^2 (2) ≈ .1 cu.ft. Then, (.1)(480) = 48 lbs.

9. (360°)(.05) - 18°

10. 4 1/16 - .006 = 4.0625 - .006 = 4.0565

11. 15 7/16" ÷ 1/8" = 247/16 . 8/1 = 123.5. Then, (123.5)(1 ft.) = 123.5 ft.

12. 7 3/8" ÷ 1/4" = 59/8 . 4/1 = 29.5 Then, (29.5)(1 ft.) = 29.5 ft.

13. (6)(4) = 24 man-days normally required. Since after 3 days only the equivalent of (2/3)(24) = 16 man-days of work has been 1 done, 8 man-days of work is still left. 16 ÷ 3 = 5 1/3, which means the crew is equivalent to only 5 1/3 men. To do the 8 man-days of work, it will require at least 8 - 5 1/3 = 2 2/3 = 3 additional men.

14. (3.5')(5')(100') = 1750 cu.ft. ≈ 64.8 cu.yds. Then, (64.8)($105) ≈ $6805

15. 2 3/8" ÷ 1/4" = 19/8 . 4/1 = 9 1/2 Then, (9 1/2)(1 ft.) = 9 1/2 feet

16. (27')(18')(1/2') = 243 cu.ft. = 9 cu.yds. (1 cu.yd. = 27 cu.ft.)

17. 2 3/4" ÷ 1/4" = 11/4 . 4/1 = 11

18. Material cost = (300)($.50) = $150. Labor cost = ($7.50)(300/5) = $450. Overhead = (.40)($150+$450) = $240. Profit = .10($150+$450+$240) = $84. Submitted price = $150 + $450 + $240 + $84 = $924

19. 6 = .57735" ÷ 8 = .0722"

20. 127 cm = 1270 mm = 1270/25.4" ≈ 50" = 4.2"

21. (25)(4.5') = 112.5' Then, (112.5X3) = 337.5 lbs.

22. (2")(2")(90") = 360 cu.in. Then, (360)(30) = 108 lbs.

23. (36')(9')(1 1/2') = 486 cu.ft. = 18 cu.yds. (1 cu.yd. = 27 cu.ft.)

24. 4 1/4" ÷ 1/2" = 17/4 . 2/1 = 8 1/2. Then, (8 1/2)(1 ft.) = 8 1/2 ft.

25. (12')(3') = 36 sq.ft. Then, (36)(60) = 2160 lbs.

TEST 3

DIRECTIONS: Each question or incomplete statement is followed by several suggested answers or completions. Select the one that BEST answers the question or completes the statement. *PRINT THE LETTER OF THE CORRECT ANSWER IN THE SPACE AT THE RIGHT.*

1. A right triangular metal sheet for a roofing job has sides of 36 inches and 4 feet. The length of the remaining side is

    A. 7 feet
    B. 6 feet
    C. 60 inches
    D. 90 inches

    1.____

2. A U.S. Standard Gauge thickness is given as 0.15625. This thickness, in fractions of an inch, is MOST NEARLY _____ inches.

    A. 1/8 B. 4/32 C. 5/32 D. 3/64

    2.____

3. The weight per 100 of sheet metal fasteners is given as 2/3 pound. The APPROXIMATE number of fasteners in a 2-pound package is

    A. 166 B. 200 C. 300 D. 266

    3.____

4. The decimal equivalent of 27/32 is MOST NEARLY

    A. 0.813 B. 0.828 C. 0.844 D. 0.859

    4.____

5. If a scaled measurement of 1'3" on the drawing of a sheet metal layout represents an actual length of 10"0", then the drawing has been made to a scale of _____ inch to the foot.

    A. 3/4 B. 1 1/4 C. 1 1/2 D. 1 3/4

    5.____

6. Two and two-thirds tees can be made from one sheet of steel. If 24 tees must be made, then the number of sheets required is

    A. 6 B. 7 C. 8 D. 9

    6.____

7. A main duct 20 inches in diameter discharges into two branch ducts. The sum of the areas of the branches is to be equal to the area of the main duct. One branch is 12 inches in diameter.
The diameter of the other branch is _____ inches.

    A. 16 B. 12 C. 10 D. 8

    7.____

8. If steel weighs 480 lbs. per cubic foot, the weight of 10 sheets, each 6 feet by 3 feet by 1/32 inch, is _____ lbs.

    A. 2,700 B. 1,237 C. 270 D. 225

    8.____

9. The area, in square inches, of a right triangle that has sides of 12 1/2, 10, and 7 1/2 inches is

    A. 18 1/4 B. 37 1/2 C. 75 D. 60

    9.____

10. In making a container to hold 1 gallon (231 cu.in.) and to be 6 inches in diameter at the top and 8 inches in diameter at the bottom, the height must be, in inches,

   A. 10.0   B. 8.2   C. 4.6   D. 6

11. A sheet metal worker is given a job to make a transition piece from a 8 1/2" diameter duct to an 11 1/4" diameter duct. If the length of the transition piece is 5 1/2" for each inch change in diameter, then the length of the transition piece is

   A. 14 7/8"   B. 15"   C. 15 1/8"   D. 15 1/4"

12. A duct layout is drawn to a scale of 3/8" to a foot. If the length of a run shown on the drawing scales 7 1/2", then the ACTUAL length of the run is

   A. 19'6"   B. 19'9"   C. 20'0"   D. 20'3"

13. An 18" x 24" duct is to be connected to a 24" x 24" duct by means of an eccentric transition piece (3 sides flush). If the taper is to be 1" in 4", then the length of the transition piece is

   A. 6"   B. 12"   C. 18"   D. 24"

14. Twenty-seven pairs of 3/8" diameter rods each 3'3 1/2" long are needed to support a duct.
   If the available rods are ten feet long, then the MINIMUM number of rods that will be needed to make the twenty-seven sets is

   A. 9   B. 12   C. 15   D. 18

15. A rectangular sheet metal air duct with open ends is 12 feet long and 15" x 20" in cross-section. If one square foot of the sheet metal weighs 1/2 pound, then the TOTAL weight of the duct is _____ lbs.

   A. 10   B. 17 1/2   C. 35   D. 150

16. The sum of 1/12 and 1/4 is

   A. 1/3   B. 5/12   C. 7/12   D. 3/8

17. The product of 12 and 2 1/3 is

   A. 27   B. 28   C. 29   D. 30

18. If 4 1/2 is subtracted from 7 1/5, the remainder is

   A. 3 7/10   B. 2 7/10   C. 3 3/10   D. 2 3/10

19. The number of cubic yards in 47 cubic feet is MOST NEARLY

   A. 1.70   B. 1.74   C. 1.78   D. 1.82

20. A wall 8'0" high by 12'6" long has a window opening 4'0" high by 3'6" wide.
   The net area of the wall (allowing for the window opening) is, in square feet,

   A. 86   B. 87   C. 88   D. 89

21. A worker's hourly rate is $11.36. 21._____
    If he works 11 1/2 hours, he should receive

    A. $129.84   B. $130.64   C. $131.48   D. $132.24

22. The number of cubic feet in 3 cubic yards is 22._____

    A. 81   B. 82   C. 83   D. 84

23. At an annual rate of $.40 per $100, what is the fire insurance premium for one year on a   23._____
    house that is insured for $80,000?

    A. $120   B. $160   C. $240   D. $320

24. A meter equals approximately 1.09 yards. 24._____
    How much longer, in yards, is a 100-meter dash than a 100-yard dash?

    A. 6   B. 8   C. 9   D. 12

25. A train leaves New York City at 8:10 A.M. and arrives in Buffalo at 4:45 P.M. on the same   25._____
    day. How long, in hours and minutes, does it take the train to make the trip?
    _____ hours, _____ minutes.

    A. 6; 22   B. 7; 16   C. 7; 28   D. 8; 35

KEY (CORRECT ANSWERS)

1. C		11. C	
2. C		12. C	
3. C		13. D	
4. C		14. D	
5. C		15. C	
6. D		16. A	
7. A		17. B	
8. D		18. B	
9. B		19. B	
10. D		20. A	

21. B
22. A
23. D
24. C
25. D

SOLUTIONS TO PROBLEMS

1. Let x = remaining side. Converting to inches, $x^2 = 36^2 + 48^2$ So, $x^2 = 3600$. Solving, x = 60 inches.

2. $.15625 = \dfrac{15,625}{100,000} = \dfrac{5}{32}$

3. $2 \div 2/3 = 3$. Then, $(3)(100) = 300$ fasteners

4. $27/32 = .84375 \approx .844$

5. 1'3" ÷ 10 = 15" ÷ 10 = 1 1/2"

6. 24 ÷ 2 2/3 = 24/1.3/8 = 9

7. Area of main duct = $(\pi)(10^2) = 100\pi$. One of the branches has an area of $(\pi)(6^2) = 36\pi$. Thus, the area of the 2nd branch = $100\pi - 36\pi = 64\pi$. The 2nd branch's radius must be 8" and its diameter must be 16".

8. Volume = (1/384')(6')(3') = .046875 cu.ft. Then, 10 sheets have a volume of .46875 cu.ft. Now, (.46875)(480) = 225 lbs.

9. Note that $(7\ 1/2)^2 + (10)^2 = (12\ 1/2)^2$, so that this is a right triangle. Area = (1/2)(10")(7 1/2") = 37 1/2 sq.in.

10. $231 = \dfrac{h}{3}[(\pi)(3)^2 + (\pi)(4)^2 + \sqrt{(9\pi)(16\pi)}]$, where h = required height. Then,

    $231 = \dfrac{h}{3}(9\pi + 16\pi + 12\pi)$. Simplifying, $231 = 37\pi h/3$.
    Solving, h ~ 5.96" or 6"

11. 11 1/4 - 8 1/2 = 2 3/4. Then, (2 3/4)(5 1/2) = 11/4 .11/2 = 15 1/8

12. 7 1/2" ÷ 3/8" = 15/2 .8/3 = 20 Then, (20)(1 ft.) = 20 feet

13. 24" - 18" = 6" Then, (6")(4) = 24"

14. 3'3 1/2" = 39.5". Now, (27)(2)(39.5") = 2133". 10 ft. = 120". Finally, 2133 ÷ 120 = 17.775, so 18 rods are needed.

15. Surface area = (2)(12')(1 1/4') + (2)(12')(1 2/3') = 70 sq.ft. Then, (70)(1/2 lb.) - 35 lbs.

16. 1/12 + 1/4 = 4/12 = 1/3

17. (12)(2 1/3) = 12/1 . 7/3 = 28

18. 7 1/5 - 4 1/2 = 7 2/10 - 4 5/10 = 6 12/10 - 4 5/10 = 2 7/10

19. 47 cu.ft. = 47/27 cu.yds. = 1.74 cu.yds.

20. (8')(12.5') - (4')(3.5') = 86 sq.ft.

21. ($11.36)(11.5) = $130.64

22. 1 cu.yd. = 27 cu.ft., so 3 cu.yds. = 81 cu.ft.

23. $80,000 ÷ $100 = 800. Then, (800)($.40) = $320

24. 100 meters = 109 yds. Then, 109 - 100 = 9 yds.

25. 4:45 P.M. - 8:10 AM. = 8 hrs. 35 min.